Presidential Racism

The Words of U.S. Presidents
Since the Civil War

And an Essay:
The Enduring Anti-Democratic
Disease Afflicting Us
—And Its Cure

ALSO BY JOHN L. HODGE

BOOKS:

Overcoming the Lie of "Race": A Personal, Philosophical, and Political Perspective (Second Edition, 2017)

Dialogues on God: Three Views (2012)

How We Are Our Enemy — And How to Stop: Our Unfinished Task of Fulfilling the Values of Democracy (2011)

Cultural Bases of Racism and Group Oppression: An Examination of Traditional "Western" Concepts, Values and Institutional Structures Which Support Racism, Sexism and Elitism (co-author) (1975)

BOOK CHAPTERS:

"Equality: Beyond Dualism and Oppression," Chapter 6 of *Anatomy of Racism* (1990)

"Democracy and Free Speech: A Normative Theory of Society and Government," Chapter 5 of *The First Amendment Reconsidered* (1982)

JOURNAL ARTICLE:

"Deadlocked-Jury Mistrials, Lesser Included Offenses, and Double Jeopardy: A Proposal to Strengthen the Manifest Necessity Requirement," *Criminal Justice Journal* (Vol. 9, No. 1) (1986)

FOR DETAILS, GO TO: JOHN L. HODGE.COM

Presidential Racism

The Words of U.S. Presidents Since the Civil War

And an Essay:

The Enduring Anti-Democratic Disease Afflicting Us —And Its Cure

John L. Hodge
J.D., Ph.D.

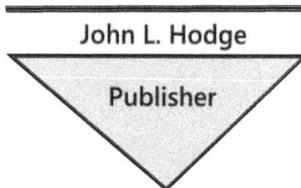

John L. Hodge

Publisher

Published in the U.S.A,
by
John L. Hodge, Publisher
Jamaica Plain, Massachusetts
U.S.A.
Email: JLHPublisher@gmail.com

Cover design and photographs by John L. Hodge.

Your comments are appreciated. Use the email address above.
Order books from local or online retailers.

**For more information,
go to the website at
johnlhodge.com**

ISBN: 978-0-9831790-7-8

Print on demand services provided by Lightning Source, Inc.

**Printed copies available through
local and online book sellers.**

CONTENTS

PREFACE

Part I of this book is both an inquiry into persistent societal norms of ancient origin that underlie the racism exemplified in Part II, and also a proposed solution based on an ethical dimension that serves as the ground for the social and cultural changes needed to overcome not only racism but also affiliated societal maladies. The racism is not only that of the presidents quoted in Part II but also that of the dominant forces of the society that put these men in office and promoted, tolerated, or turned a blind eye to the racist policies that ensued. The presidents, in turn, reinforced that society-wide racism through statements and policies that rippled throughout the society. It is notable that the racist views of 2020 differ little from those of 1866.

I wrote the essay that is in Part I—the result of many decades of research, observation and thought*--and put it here, because it seemed unfair to leave the reader only with the troubling questions and disgust that naturally emerge from Part II without analysis and proposed direction for the future. I hope you will read both parts to understand the enormous depth of the problem with which we are faced. Racism is an imbedded part of the bigger problem of human

---

* This essay incorporates and builds upon ideas that I first presented in *Cultural Bases of Racism and Group Oppression: An Examination of Traditional "Western" Concepts, Values and Institutional Structures Which Support Racism, Sexism and Elitism*, by John L. Hodge, Donald K. Struckmann and Lynn Dorland Trost (Berkeley, CA: Two Riders Press, 1975) and developed further in my writings cited in the essay.

inequality.

Many like to slough off the problem by assigning it to human nature. This is always a conservative reaction designed to accept atrocities and do nothing. Real human nature, on the other hand, comprehends all of its facets, including every effort to change and improve the lot of humankind. Real human nature is a work in progress and is not only what the past has wrought but also our aspirations and efforts to create a better future.

John L. Hodge
Jamaica Plain, Massachusetts
July 15, 2020

(Note: The texts of all internet links cited in this book were tested and correct at the time of publication.)

PART I

THE ENDURING ANTI-DEMOCRATIC DISEASE AFFLICTING US —AND ITS CURE

The Enduring Anti-Democratic Disease Afflicting Us —And Its Cure

The world is plagued with anti-democratic institutions, beliefs and behavior. These institutions, beliefs and behavior form an interactive complex that prevents real democracy from being attained.

That we call nations "democracies" in spite of these anti-democratic forces is deceptive and false. These nations are all partial democracies teetering on a wall separating progress towards real democracy on one side and tyranny or chaos on the other.

The United States is no exception. Part II of this book documents the United States' ongoing legacy of white supremacy, one of the major impediments to real democracy.

Real democracy is more than a right to vote and have representatives elected by a majority. It is a way of life based on the concept of human equality. Anti-democratic forces arise from a disease that undermines equality and enables small elites to have excessive power.

As for elections, the elites decide or heavily influence what any pool of candidates will be—though their power goes far beyond elections. In the United States, these elites consist mostly of those with enormous wealth who comprise a very small percentage of the population. The general population believes that when they vote, they are freely choosing their representatives and the president, but their choices are largely determined or heavily influenced without their input. Most of the people who have chosen to run for office are either wealthy themselves,* have the support of those who are wealthy, or obtained a prior important office or position though the support of those who are wealthy. There are exceptions, but that there are exceptions demonstrates that they are not the norm.

But the anti-democratic disease is much more than a political disease. Anti-democratic institutions pervade the entire society and include economic, educational, and religious institutions. This disease infects not only the society but also, in varying degrees, the beliefs and habits of each individual. It is within us as well as outside around us. What is within us and outside us interact and sustain each other.

The anti-democratic disease has many devastating and recognizable symptoms. Among them are beliefs and behaviors such as racism, sexism, homophobia, religious intolerance, xenophobia, tribalism, and nationalism. But the disease also generates and sustains anti-democratic institutions that support these beliefs and behaviors, just as these beliefs and behaviors support these institutions. These institutions include economic institutions—largely private corporations—that are designed to accumulate wealth to increase the wealth of a small minority, and legal structures that permit this wealth to flow into and manipulate public

---

* In 2018, fifty-two United States Senators (52%) each had a net worth of one million dollars or more and an average per senator net worth of over nine million dollars. https://www.rollcall.com/wealth-of-congress/ . In contrast, in 2016 the bottom 50% of U.S. families had a median net worth of $40,000, and the bottom 25% had a median net worth of $200. The *mean* net worth of the bottom 25% was negative. *Federal Reserve Bulletin*, Sept., 2017 (Vol. 103, No. 3), p. 13; https://www.federalreserve.gov/publications/files/scf17.pdf .

and political policies. These legal structures favor those with considerable wealth, because those with considerable wealth have disproportionate say in creating these structures.

Throughout human history, societies and personal relationships that have been nourished by the concept of human equality have also been infected by this anti-democratic disease. This disease has a common source, a mostly subconscious force that I call *ingrained elitism*.

What is it and what makes it a disease?

The Foundation of Health

That this anti-democratic force is a disease presupposes a concept of health. Health derives from the idea of equality that is implicit in the properly interpreted Golden Rule.* Broadly stated, the Golden Rule means to treat others as you would want them to treat you. This idea and its practice is the foundation of personal as well as societal health.

The Golden Rule is not some consequence of rational necessity or a commandment imposed from Above. Instead, it is a belief that seems to make sense, as many others have found. Versions of the Golden Rule have been expressed throughout history and all over the world as the core of ethical living. Its widespread acceptance is a starting point for recommending it.† But there is more to the Golden Rule

---

* The incorrect interpretations and objections of Immanuel Kant and Herman Melville are refuted in my book, *How We Are Our Enemy — And How to Stop: Our Unfinished Task of Fulfilling the Values of Democracy* (Jamaica Plain, Mass.: John L. Hodge, Publisher, 2011), pp. 142 – 147.

† See Jeffrey Wattles, *The Golden Rule* (New York and Oxford: Oxford Univ. Press, 1996).

than what it initially appears to be.

The Golden Rule presumes that you and the other have something in common in spite of observable differences. The thing in common is not visible. It is our inviolate interiority. Awareness of this interiority probably precedes recorded history. Ancient texts and inscriptions often refer to it as "soul," which is a pre-religious idea that need not be conflated with immortality or separation from the body. The other source of the Golden Rule is empathy, which also presupposes that the other has an interiority like our own.

The Golden Rule is usually hemmed in by the view that it refers only to local or bilateral personal interactions, say, of you to your neighbor. The anti-democratic disease imposes this limitation. But logically it is not so limited. It is not only the foundation for healthy personal living among your neighbors but also the foundation of a healthy, democratic society and a healthy world.

This is because the Golden Rule and the idea of human equality are necessarily connected. The idea of equality is implicit in the idea that you treat another as you would want to be treated. It means that you treat the other as equal to you, as neither inferior nor superior. But this equality is not limited to you and the other, but extends also to an other not known to you but known to the other. The equality of the other known to you to the other not known to you connects your equality to the other not known to you.

To see this more clearly, begin with the assumption that you believe in the Golden Rule as applicable not only to yourself but as something others should follow. Add to this the transitive rule in mathematics. According to the transitive rule, if A=B and B=C, then A=C. If you are A and an other known to you is B, your belief in the Golden Rule establishes your equality to B, so A=B. If B knows C, your belief that others should follow the Golden Rule establishes B's equality to C, so B=C. Due to these equalities established by your belief in the Golden Rule, A=B and also B=C, and under the transitive rule, therefore, A=C. Once this triadic equality of A, B and C is acknowledged, then the equality connects indefinitely to others. If C knows D, C=D; under the transitive rule, A=D. Due to the Golden Rule, if D knows E, then D=E; under the transitive rule, A=E. And so on. Equality has no limits. You may never have met C, D, or E. They could be completely unknown to you. The transitive rule makes explicit what is implicit in your belief: that the equality that is presumed between A and B now extends to C, D, and E, and beyond without limit. Thus, your belief in the Golden Rule logically contains within it the concept of your equality to everyone, a universal equality.

The transitive rule is essential to understanding why the Golden Rule is a political, economic and social concept as well as a personal one. It logically leads to the concept of human equality, that all people are of equal humanity and worth. This concept, in turn, is the foundation of democracy, a political idea that requires that every person be enabled to have an equal voice in creating the government and society in which they live. Accordingly, this extension of the Golden Rule – the original Golden Rule extended by the transitive rule – I will call the Extended Golden Rule.

The Extended Golden Rule*

The transitive rule is the logical, mathematical component that transforms a belief in the Golden Rule into the Extended Golden Rule. But the Extended Golden Rule is more than a rational concept; it opens the door to the

---

* I previously called this "the golden guide" in *How We Are our Enemy – And How to Stop*, pp.147 ff.

discovery of the vitality of living. This discovery occurs, because your belief in the equality of an other opens your mind and heart to actually experiencing the equal humanity of the other. The wonderfulness of that experience, in turn, reinforces your belief in equality and encourages you to extend your belief to the equality of all others, including others whom you had not met before and others whom you will never meet but with whom you connect through empathy.* The Extended Golden Rule removes all barriers to empathy. The experience of the vitality of living is then freed to flow into your being.

Reinforced by these experiences, the Extended Golden Rule does not need faith or rational proof to be the ethical foundation of how you live.

Those who block these experiences with fear reinforced by their beliefs in their own greater righteousness or superiority lose out. To sustain these false beliefs, they latch onto ideologies and myths that block empathy and disable their ability to experience the equal humanity of others. Others become objects to be oppressed or disparaged and maybe killed. The anti-democratic disease, explained below, is itself rooted in a largely unconscious equality-destroying mythology.

The Essence of Equality and the Necessity of Human Rights

But what is this equality? It does not mean that you are the same as the other. You do not look like the other. You have different relationships. You have different circumstances. You are unique and different from everyone

---

* The relevance of empathy is nicely portrayed in Lynn Hunt, *Inventing Human Rights* (New York: W.W. Norton, 2007).

else. This means that equality is different from sameness.

The core of our equality is our inviolate interiority which everyone has yet is unique in each individual. This inviolate interiority includes everything we experience, including our emotions, feelings, thoughts and sensations. It also includes our decision-making power and the decisions that minute by minute influence what we do and our impact on the world outside of ourselves.

Thus, this inviolate interiority does not remain hidden somewhere within. It manifests itself through expression in the outer world: actions, speech, writings, art, inventions, discovery, creations, connections to others. Without these expressions, our inviolate interiority would be imprisoned, depressed and sad. Authorities often seek to deny it or suppress it, for it is a threat to them.

The expressions of one person can lead to conflict with the expressions of others. A social adjustment is needed to coordinate these expressions so that the expressions of some do not oppress the expressions of others. Our core equality is meaningless if some are enslaved, oppressed or killed by others who enjoy wealth and prosperity. Equality requires a common ground that protects us and enables our inviolate interiority to express itself in the world in a way that respects the inviolate interiority of everyone.

This common ground is implicit in and protected by the concept of human rights. Human rights are not only individual rights but also the underlying governing principles of democratic societies. Human rights, while pertaining to the individual, incorporate the social principle of *equal rights*. They are the foundation of the protection of our inviolate interiority from external abuse.

Human rights evolve over time as growing agreements about what constitutes the common core of our equality such that it deserves protection *by* government as well as protection *from* government. Laws protecting individuals from unfair discrimination are an example of protection by government. Laws protecting freedom of speech against governmental restrictions are an example of freedom from government. Regarding human rights as "natural rights" misses the point and begs the question, because "natural rights" too depend on human agreements about what constitutes the equality component of what is natural.

An international and cross-cultural agreement about these rights is the Universal Declaration of Human Rights adopted in 1948 by the United Nations General Assembly (reproduced here in the Appendix). Forty-eight nations from all regions of the globe, including the United States, voted to adopt it. The purpose of these rights, as stated in its Preamble, includes affirming "the dignity and worth of the human person and in the equal rights of men and women." Without human rights, majority rule is a form of tyranny that enables any majority to oppress any minority, just as rule by an elite is tyranny over the majority. Healthy societies, thus, require human rights as their foundation. Without human rights, the idea of equality is undermined and violated.

Human rights are about societal health as well as individual health. Every society contains individuals who see flaws in the society and look for ways to improve it. They dissent from the status quo. Human rights protect dissenters from abuse by those who object to change, just as human rights equally protect everyone from dissidents if they become abusive or violent. By protecting peaceful but expressive dissenters, human rights facilitate the expression of new ideas and efforts that enable a society to progress and not stagnate.

Some propose that the ideal society is unified and harmonized with everyone playing the same pleasant tune. Those who seek to play something more interesting would be castigated. Such a society would be oppressive and devoid of the protections human rights provide to those who propose change. Often some discord is needed to jar a society out of its slumber.

Equality based in human rights is not about uniformity or the suppression of individual uniqueness. It is about the dignity and worth of all human beings as unique individuals. Enforced conformity disrespects dissenters, and, thus, is contrary to human rights. A harmonized society is necessarily repressive of individual uniqueness.

The freedom of the individual is justifiably constrained whenever that freedom can be demonstrated (not merely asserted) to endanger the well-being of others. The appropriate degree of constraint is not some theoretical constant but varies with circumstances — for example, in a crowd or during a pandemic. Unfettered individualism — pure freedom — would allow individuals to suppress or deny human rights to others. As R. H. Tawney put it, "Freedom for the pike is death to the minnows."* Unconstrained freedom of the individual is not a societal virtue. The equality of all means that each individual respects and affirms the equal worth and humanity of every individual. This equality is the legitimate constraint on individualism, yet it is a constraint that affirms the individual as a unique being, free to voice dissent, and also equal to others.

The process whereby individuals support one another as unique and equal individuals is a social process. Individuals engaged in this process work to create and sustain a society that supports the equality and uniqueness of all individuals. This work necessarily brings them into conflict with the components of existing societies that are oppressive and support inequality.

---

* *Equality* (London: George Allen & Unwin, 1964), p. 164 (first published in 1931).

The anti-democratic disease, which I will examine below, counteracts equality and prevents the fulfillment of human rights. None of the nations that voted for the Universal Declaration of Human Rights has yet succeeded in fully incorporating these rights into national policy. The United States, for example, has as of this writing failed to enact the proposed Equal Rights Amendment to the U.S. Constitution, which would guarantee equal rights for women. The United States, like many nations of the world, also fails to fulfill Article 25 of this Declaration (among others), which states in part, "Everyone has the right to a standard of living adequate for the health and well-being of himself and of his family, including food, clothing, housing and medical care and necessary social services." In the U.S., poverty, homelessness and lack of adequate health care plague much of the society. In addition to racism, misogyny, and exclusionary immigration policies resulting from religious and racial animosities, the United States, like most countries of the world, is thoroughly infected with the anti-democratic disease, and has been since it was founded as a nation that embraced slavery and the oppression of women.

Expressions of the Anti-Democratic Disease

Intellectual history reveals the source of presumptions that are passed on from generation to generation, usually sufficiently beneath awareness to evade scrutiny. We must delve deeply into this history to uncover the anti-democratic disease.

To find evidence of the anti-democratic disease, we have to look no further than the stated beliefs of the people historically honored as famous men. In the European and European-influenced parts of the world (including the

United States and former European colonies around the world), these famous men include Plato, Aristotle, St. Augustine, Martin Luther, John Calvin, Immanuel Kant, and Sigmund Freud. They make suitable examples of the disease. Ingrained in their world-views, as well as in the views of many others who are honored, we find blatant racism, sexism, and elitism. Sexism is one of its key ingredients.

For example, Plato said, "The greatest number and variety of desires and pleasures and pains is generally to be found in children and women and slaves, and in the less respectable majority of so-called free men." Aristotle said, "The male is by nature superior, and the female inferior; and the one rules, and the other is ruled; this principle, of necessity, extends to all mankind." The early Christian theologian Saint Augustine, who advocated celibacy for men to avoid the pollution of women, said, "He who is unmarried is concerned with God's claim, asking how he is to please God; whereas the married man is concerned with the world's claim, asking how he is to please his wife." The Protestant reformer Martin Luther said, "A wife ought to be obedient to her husband as her lord, be subject to him, yield to him, keep silent and agree with him as long as it is not contrary to God." Protestant reformer John Calvin said, "Wives cannot obey Christ unless they yield obedience to their husbands." The famous philosopher Immanuel Kant said that a woman's "philosophy is not to reason, but to sense." "I hardly believe that the fair sex is capable of principles." The famous psychologist Sigmund Freud said, "Women soon come into opposition to civilization and display their retarding and restraining influence. . . . The work of civilization has become increasingly the business of men, it confronts them with ever more difficult tasks and compels them to carry out instinctual sublimations of which women are little capable."*

The "civilization" of which Freud speaks is hierarchically structured around inequality, with men yielding power over women. Freud instructs women to "choose her husband for his paternal characteristics and . . . recognize his authority."† With these words, Freud expressed the views of over two thousand years of European intellectual and religious history, where men rule and are supposed to rule over women.

This "civilization" is also racist. Just as Immanuel Kant did in the late eighteenth century, Freud in the twentieth century affirmed the superiority of the European or "white" race: "Leadership of the human species" has fallen upon the "great ruling powers among the white nations."‡ Freud

---

* Plato, *The Republic,* trans. D. Lee, 2nd ed. (Baltimore: Penguin Books, 1974), p. 202. Aristotle, *Politics,* 1254b, in *The Basic Works of Aristotle,* ed. R. McKeon (New York: Random House, 1941) pp. 1132. St. Augustine, *Confessions,* Bk. II, #2, trans. R. S. Pine-Coffin (Baltimore: Penguin, 1961), p. 44. Martin Luther, "Treatise on Good Works," trans. W. A. Lambert, revised by J. Atkinson, *Luther's Works,* v. 44 (Philadelphia: Fortress, 1966), p. 98. John Calvin, *The Epistle to the Ephesians,* 5:22; contained in *Calvin's Commentaries: The Epistles of Paul the Apostle to the Galatians, Ephesians, Philippians and Colossians,* trans. T. H. L. Parker (London: Oliver & Boyd, 1965). Immanuel Kant, *Observations on the Feeling of the Beautiful and Sublime,* trans. J. T. Goldthwait (Berkeley, CA: Univ. of California Press, 1960), pp. 79, 81. Sigmund Freud, *Civilization and Its Discontents,* trans. James Strachey (New York: W. W. Norton, 1962), pp. 50-51.

† *An Outline of Psycho-Analysis,* trans. James Strachey (New York: W. W. Norton, 1949), p. 51.

‡ "Reflections upon War and Death," trans. E. Colburn Mayne, in *Character and Culture,* ed. Paul Rieff (New York: Collier Books, 1963), p. 108; also see p. 113. See Freud, *Totem and Taboo* (New York: W. W. Norton, 1950), pp. 2, 3 n.2, 12 ff, 40-41, 54 & 139. See

viewed the non-"white" peoples of the world similarly to the way he viewed women—as people not capable of controlling their instincts and who therefore should be ruled by those who can. Thus, European colonialism is viewed not as the brutal, exploitative system that it was but as the proper order of things.

Ironically, Freud had to escape from the Nazis even though they shared a common view of civilization as consisting of the inferiority of women and the superiority of a so-called "white race" of which Freud saw himself as a member. This view of civilization is thoroughly ingrained in our culture, as indicated by the continued honoring of these famous men throughout much of the educational system.*

The inequality of men and women and the view of the superiority of men was openly advocated by these honored men, and, in addition, Immanuel Kant and Sigmund Freud openly advocated European or "white" supremacy. While apologists try to separate out the flaws in these honored thinkers from the rest of their views, they are blind to the idea that these flaws are a part of an overall framework of hierarchical thinking that assumed the inequality of people and the innate superiority of some over others. There was no room for democracy in their schemes. To honor them (as opposed to studying them due to their influence) and to advocate for democracy is a contradiction.

Immanuel Kant, *Education*, trans. A. Churton (Ann Arbor: Ann Arbor Paperbacks, 1960), p. 4.

* A thorough examination of the views of Plato, St. Augustine, Luther, Calvin, and Freud is contained in John L. Hodge, D. K. Struckmann & L. D. Trost, *Cultural Bases of Racism and Group Oppression* (Berkeley, CA: Two Riders Press, 1975), pp. 97ff and 123ff. A condensed version of this examination that added Immanuel Kant is contained in John L. Hodge, *How We Are Our Enemy — And How to Stop*, pp. 42 ff.

The Anti-Democratic Disease: Ingrained Elitism

These honored men expressed the view that society should consist of hierarchical inequality. Men are viewed as superior to women. The so-called "white race" is viewed as superior to others. This superiority is not just conceptual. It is assumed that this superiority entitles the superior to rule the inferior. It is the formula supporting unequal societies governed by ingrained elites. This way of thinking is the anti-democratic disease.

An essential feature of this diseased way of thinking is that the major components of the hierarchy are ingrained — that is, either unchangeable or changeable only with significant difficulty. One's position in the hierarchy is largely determined by factors over which individuals have little or no control. Whether you were observed at birth as male or female cannot be changed. Though some become transgendered, any transition made later is difficult and attempted only by a relative few. Similarly, whether you are classified as "white" at birth or not "white" cannot be changed. Though some who are initially classified as not "white" are able to change that classification later, they are able to do so only if they have a certain appearance, and relatively few take the additional effort to do so. Those born with wealth are likely to stay wealthy; those born in poverty are likely to stay in poverty, and the exceptions do not alter these likelihoods. The hierarchy is either determined or largely determined. As Aristotle stated in his advocacy of hierarchy, "For that some should rule and others be ruled is a thing not only necessary, but expedient; from the hour of their birth, some are marked out for subjection, others for rule."*

---

* *Politics*, 1254b; contained in *The Basic Works of Aristotle*, ed. Richard McKeon (New York: Random House, 1941), p. 1132.

The hierarchical structure of society is, in turn, a component of a larger view of the entire universe as a mostly or completely pre-determined hierarchical distribution of beings. This view of the universe was exposed by Arthur O. Lovejoy in his book, *The Great Chain of Being*.* The Great Chain of Being "was the conception of the plan and structure of the world which, through the Middle Ages and down to the late eighteenth century, many philosophers, most men of science, and, indeed, most educated men, were to accept without question – the conception of the universe as a 'Great Chain of Being,' composed of an immense, or . . . of an infinite, number of links ranging in hierarchical order from the meagerest kind of existents . . . to the highest possible kind of creature."† Lovejoy, however, could perceptively see the past but did not see how embedded this hierarchical conception remains in present-day culture.

In addition, Lovejoy did not draw out the full political relevance of the Great Chain of Being as being not simply a metaphysical or theological ranking but a justification for a hierarchical distribution of power that entitles those higher in the order to rule over those who are lower. Accompanying the belief in the hierarchical order of the universe was the idea that those lower in the hierarchy exist to serve those higher. After all, why else would God create the lower beings? Implicit in this idea of service is the idea that those higher in the hierarchy have a right and even a duty to compel such service. Thus, service by those lower translates into power over the lower by those who are higher. The hierarchical distribution of power is a chain of command. The Great Chain of Being is a political tool favoring those in power whereby those at the top have the

* (New York: Harper & Bros., 1960) (originally published in 1936).
† *Ibid, p.* 59.

greatest power and those at the bottom are the subjects of
those above, where the purpose of those who are lower is to
serve those who are higher. Political authority and
theological authority thus unite in perpetuating a concept
that supports the power of some over others.

This implicit chain of command is why this paradigm of
the universe requires social and political hierarchies. In
tracing practices that led to the acceptance of slavery in the
land that became the United States, historian Betty Wood
described sixteenth and early seventeenth century England
as "characterized by a strong sense of hierarchy." "The
Great Chain of Being provided theoretical support for the
proposition that social rank was predetermined and
unalterable, that some were born to be gentlemen and to
govern while others, the majority, were fated to be poor and
to provide labor, and this was the actuality of life. . . ."* The
idea translated into the structuring of daily life. The slavery
that emerged subsequently in America fit neatly into this
hierarchical scheme and fortified the racism that continued
after slavery and plagues America and much of the world
today.

Although the Great Chain of Being may seem to be
nothing more than an abstract ancient idea with little
practical relevance today, instead it is thoroughly
embedded in our current way of life. The distinction
between mind and body becomes mind over body; the mind
should rule. The distinction between reason and emotion
becomes reason over emotion; reason should dominate over
emotion. The difference between male and female becomes
male (or to some, female) superiority. Differences of skin
color mean that one is better than the other. Differences
among nations and cultures mean that some are superior to

---

* Betty Wood, *The Origins of American Slavery* (New York: Hill and
Wang, 1997), p. 13.

others and that the superior should dominate the others and coerce them into service. The rich are seen as superior to the poor and should have more power. In all facets of our lives we seek out and honor who is best and ignore or belittle the necessary contributions of others who are under-appreciated. The educational system typically ranks students through a grading system and demeans those towards the bottom. Revolutionaries may seek to turn the vertical hierarchy upside down, creating another hierarchy with themselves at the top, while ignoring the notion of a mostly horizontal society with some flexible rounded hills and gentle slopes. The presumption of hierarchy means that we are generally inclined to see most things dualistically as either above or below other things, and thus separated from one another, and are less inclined to see different things as together side by side. Our default way of thinking is that of separateness, "either/or," not of togetherness, "both/and."*
The Great Chain of Being is the underlying premise that is everywhere so we do not see it. But we must see it to address its pervasive influence.

Lovejoy traces the idea of The Great Chain of Being back 2400 years to Plato and Aristotle, the two men still regarded today in academia as the primary philosophers at the root of "Western" civilization. But these philosophers also fed the roots of sexism, racism and elitism, also prominent features of "Western" civilization (and elsewhere). Plato's hierarchy placed rationality at the top, emotions at the bottom. This set the stage for the culturally ingrained dualism of mind and body, reason and emotion. His pupil Aristotle said, "For that which can foresee by the exercise of mind is by nature intended to be lord and master, and that which can with its body give effect to such foresight is a

---

* I described this as a feature of Dualist culture in *Cultural Bases of Racism and Group Oppression*, Part VI.

subject, and by nature a slave."* Thus, he asserts social hierarchy as necessary, with physical laborers at the bottom. His predecessor, Plato, set forth the concept of social hierarchy in *The Republic*, wherein he asserts with his Divided Line that society must be ruled by an intellectual elite, philosopher-kings, for the majority of humankind are governed by passion and emotion, which is unsuitable for governing.

These views underlie modern societies. Physical laborers, identified with the body, are paid less, even though their work is as essential to the functioning of society as corporate executives, identified with the mind, who get paid hundreds or thousands times more. Women and people identified as "black" are viewed as more emotional than men and people identified as "white" are seen disproportionately as the holders of reason. The idea of reason over emotion prevails.† Accordingly, our society is Aristotelian at its core.

Freud incorporated this hierarchy of reason over emotion into the human psyche, postulating an id as the holder of passion and emotion that must be controlled by developed superegos. He identified the rational superego with the European male who has the task of maintaining control over the id of women and non-Europeans. This hierarchy, to him, is the very foundation of civilization.‡

The fallacy of this hierarchy of reason over emotion was succinctly exposed by Jose Ortega y Gasset: "A moral

---

* *Politics*, 1252a; contained in *The Basic Works of Aristotle*, ed. Richard McKeon (New York: Random House, 1941), p. 1128.

† This is thoroughly analyzed in Hodge, et al., *Cultural Bases of Racism and Group Oppression*.

‡ See Freud, *Civilization and its Discontents* and the analysis of Freud's views in Hodge, et al., *Cultural Bases of Racism and Group Oppression*, Part IV, Section 5.

system which is geometrically perfect but leaves us cold and is no spur to action is subjectively immoral. The ethical ideal cannot content itself with being the most correct of ideals: it must also succeed in arousing our emotions."* Instead of this emotionless Platonic ideal form of truth and the good, mind and body, reason and emotion, superego and id must function together on the same level as equal partners.

Social hierarchy, thus, is not just something that happens through exercise of might but is seen as something that ought to happen, with an ingrained elite as rulers or administrators. Throughout history this kind of hierarchy has been assumed to be the ideal of social order. This assumption is reflected today in our social structure and institutions and penetrates throughout our culture, as further explained below. The ideal of hierarchy is a pervasive ideology, ingrained in our mostly unconscious way of thinking, connecting the ancient past to the present and standing in the way of progress towards a more humane future.

Ingrained Hierarchy Today--Wealthocracy

Against this history of the ideal of ingrained hierarchical social order has emerged the idea of democracy based on the idea of human equality. Ingrained hierarchy, which incorporates ingrained elitism, and human equality are necessarily in conflict.

The conflict was apparent from the beginning of the founding of the United States. The 1776 American Declaration of Independence courageously announced the

---

* *The Modern Theme*, trans. J. Cleugh (New York: Harper Torchbooks, 1961), p. 48 (originally published in 1923 as *Tema de nuestro tiempo*).

idea of human equality, and several paragraphs later spoke of "the merciless Indian savages." The celebrated American Revolution was fought and won, because the North joined with the South when the South's purpose for entering the war was to preserve slavery and protect itself from the English court decision, *Somerset* v. *Stewart*,* which had effectively ended slavery in England four years before the signing of the Declaration.† The July 4th celebrations are, in effect, a celebration of continued slavery. The power of the South continued after the Revolution. The U.S. Constitution provided that certain people not regarded as "white" be counted as three-fifth of a person for the purpose of determining representation in the House of Representatives,‡ giving the South greater per-capita representation of free people than in the North. Furthermore, slavery was permitted by the U.S. Constitution, and after the Constitution was ratified, slavery continued for over seven decades until the Civil War. Slaves were defined by the laws of many southern states not as people but as property. Thus, they were not three-fifths of a person except for counting purposes; they were zero-fifths of a person for all other purposes. After slavery ended, many states, particularly in the South, enacted laws that separated "whites" from non-"whites." These apartheid laws (called "Jim Crow" and "segregation") were not fully abolished until 1967 when the U.S. Supreme Court decided that states cannot prohibit "interracial" marriages.§

The U.S. Constitution, when it became effective in 1789,

---

* 98 ER 499; 12 Geo. 3 (1772)

† See Alfred W. Blumrosen & Ruth G. Blumrosen, *Slave Nation* (Naperville, Ill.: Sourcebooks, 2005).

‡ United States Constitution, Art. I, Sec. 2, para. 3.

§ *Loving* v. *Virginia*, 388 U.S. 1 (1967).

contradicted the idea of human equality, revealing the strength of the enduring anti-democratic disease and its source, the Great Chain of Being. Remarkably, and widely misunderstood today, the U.S. Constitution did not grant to anyone the right to vote and still does not require universal suffrage.* The right to vote was left to the states, and the states then confined this right to an ingrained elite of property-owning "white" males until some states later broadened the franchise. The 15th Amendment (1870) to the Constitution, worded negatively, does not create a right to vote but only says that whatever right to vote that might exist cannot be denied "on account of race, color, or previous condition of servitude." Members of the U.S. Senate were not elected by popular vote until 1913 with the ratification of the 17th Amendment — but at that time women could be excluded from any right to vote. The right to vote contained in state laws was permitted to be confined to males until 1920 with the enactment of the 19th Amendment. Today, the popular vote still does not elect the President. That task is assigned to electors who are chosen under various state laws. Presidents George W. Bush and Donald Trump both lost the national popular vote and were selected by electors.

As Alexander Keyssar documented, "The principle of 'one person, one vote' — and its underlying presumption that the votes of all individuals should count equally — does not yet apply to presidential elections. . . . According to the Supreme Court . . . presidential electors [ ] need not be chosen by popular vote at all."† The conservative judicial ideology maintaining that the constitutionality of a law depends on what the framers intended is itself a product of

---

* Alexander Keyssar, *The Right to Vote* (New York: Basic Books, 2000), pp. 4, 317, 329.
† *The Right to Vote*, p. 328.

the anti-democratic disease, *for the framers of the U.S. Constitution did not create or intend to create a democracy.*

The consequences of the non-democratic and even anti-democratic U.S. Constitution are apparent today. Police patrol many "black" neighborhoods as an occupation force and brutalize or kill their occupants without being convicted of assault or murder. Protestors and news reporters are shot and injured with rubber bullets, with the implicit threat that the next time the rubber may be replaced with lead. People who live in the United States today who are not U.S. citizens are, in varying degrees depending on their status, denied fundamental human rights. People who are considered to be present illegally have none of the human rights protections that should be accorded to all people. They have been imprisoned and often deported without the due process of law that citizens are entitled to. Migrants seeking to enter the United States from Mexico have been incarcerated by U.S. agents under inhumane and brutal conditions; young children have been taken from their parents. These are gross violations of human rights, but no international court has assumed the power to convict the United States of its crimes against humanity.

In the United States, the political power yielded by the extremely wealthy contrasts sharply with the subservient position of the poor. Although it is possible for a poor or middle-class person to become wealthy, and some do, overall the wealthy are an ingrained elite where wealth is passed on to their children. Rising out of poverty is very difficult and possible only for a tiny few. Many accept the idea that the poor deserve to be poor and should not be given any benefits that might help them emerge from poverty. Many would even deny them health care.

This power yielded by the wealthy, however, is not an anomaly. Instead, it is what the framers of the Constitution intended. This country was founded on the belief that the propertyless should have little or no say in what the government is or does. Today it follows from that belief that those with the most wealth should have the most say.

While the framers wisely created a barrier between religion and government, they did not and did not intend to create a barrier protecting government from concentrated wealth. Such protection could begin with protecting the electoral process from the influence of concentrated wealth, for this process depends on campaign contributions that largely determine who the elected officials will be. Such a protection must be created if real democracy is to be attained.

Building a barrier that protects government from religion was relatively simple and accomplished within a single sentence of the First Amendment that prevents Congress from passing any law respecting any religion. Preventing concentrated wealth from influencing campaigns for elected government office is more difficult and requires creative legislation developed over time involving trial and error. Congress and many state legislatures were engaged in making such legislation, but the U.S. Supreme Court effectively blocked these efforts by declaring that expenditures for political campaigns was a form of free speech protected by the First Amendment, and further declared that corporations could also "speak" with money.* In some respects this seems ludicrous, but, on the other hand, the U.S. Supreme Court logically continued what the framers created, a legal framework where wealth in the form of property, including shares of corporations, provides its owners with rights and privileges that others should not have, including the right to influence and

---

* *Citizens United* v. *Federal Election Commission*, 558 U.S. 310 (2010).

determine the makeup of the government.*

Thus a constitutional amendment will be needed to override the Supreme Court's decision and enable federal and state legislatures to find ways to create legal barriers preventing concentrated wealth from dominating the electoral process and thereby shaping the government. Such an amendment might read like this: "The legislative power of Congress and of each state shall include the power to make laws that regulate direct or indirect expenditures for any political campaign for any state or federal office, including expenditures by candidates supporting their own campaigns, and may provide for exclusive public sources of campaign financing, provided that such expenditures or financing are sufficient to insure reasonable and fair public exposure for all candidates." †

In spite of the daring, historic words that introduced the Declaration, the anti-democratic disease infected everything that followed, even in the Declaration itself. What the U.S. Constitution created was not a democracy but a wealthocracy, a society in which the wealthy have the greatest influence and get the greatest benefit. The Constitution will have to be amended to remove its own impediment to real democracy. This will be difficult to achieve but necessary if real democracy is to be attained, even though by itself such an amendment will not end racism and sexism — which must end.

---

* I criticized this approach and proposed an alternative long before *Citizens United* was decided: "Democracy and Free Speech: A Normative Theory of Society and Government," Chapter 5 of *The First Amendment Reconsidered*, ed. B. F. Chamberlin & C. J. Brown (New York and London: Longman, 1982).

† That a corporation is a legal "person" has been settled law since the nineteenth century and is not the primary problem. The primary problem is the role of wealth concentrated from any source, including biological persons as well as legal persons.

Democratic and Anti-Democratic Hierarchies

There are three essential kinds of hierarchies of relevance here.

- Ingrained hierarchies of power, where those at the top are an ingrained elite who have power over those below;
- Hierarchies of simple ranking which do not involve power or lead to power later;
- Democratic hierarchies which involve the granting of power that is temporary and not ingrained.

The absence of any hierarchy is not a sensible option for society or personal living. Hierarchies of simple ranking, which do not involve power, are necessary and useful guides. When you make a grocery list and state first and second choices in case the first choice is not available or too expensive, you are creating a hierarchy of ranking. In sports, players are ranked and compete as part of the game. As long as a player at the top has no power to win aside from skill at playing the game, ranking is part of the fun of the sport and has no political implications. Hierarchies of ranking are not always harmless, however, as many such hierarchies are intertwined with ingrained hierarchies of power.

Hierarchies of power go beyond simple ranking and involve the power of those above over those below. But unlike ingrained hierarchies of power, in democratic hierarchies power is temporary and subject to continual redistribution. To accomplish specific tasks, hierarchies are useful when leaders are chosen to help guide and coordinate others, or when representatives are chosen to express what others want. Such hierarchies are necessary to minimize chaos and to enable effective action. In democratic hierarchies, however, the power of leaders is granted to them temporarily by those who have chosen to be led. Those who have chosen to be led retain the power to change the leaders, and no power is granted to the leaders that could enable them to maintain themselves in positions of leadership. If a leader seeks to use the position of leadership to remain as leader contrary to the desires of those led, the leader has become corrupt and must be removed.

Ingrained hierarchies are ingrained largely because they are hierarchies of power that give those with power the ability to maintain themselves in control. Democratic hierarchies are transient, subject to the desire of those who are led, whereas ingrained hierarchies continue with minimal regard to those who are led. Democratic hierarchies embody the idea of human equality. Ingrained hierarchies assume and perpetuate inequality.

Corporations are typically controlled by shareholders in proportion to the number of shares they own, making them hierarchies of power based on wealth. The largest shareholders of large corporations are generally members of the ingrained elite, a few of whom have joined recently and will remain due to their enormous wealth.

The goal of creating real democracies, thus, includes the goal of replacing ingrained hierarchies with democratic hierarchies or regulating ingrained hierarchies to serve the public.

How These Historical Forces Divide Us

The contradiction between the idea of democracy based on human equality and the idea of a hierarchical society ruled by ingrained elites is played out today in countries that are called "democracies." The United States is not an exception but a prime example of this contradiction.

One expression of this contradiction is the visible division of the United States into two Americas. One commentator, John Blake, summed up the conflict: "These two Americas have long co-existed. One is the country represented by the Statue of Liberty, and its invitation to poor and tired immigrants 'yearning to breathe free.' The other is the one that virtually wiped out Native Americans, enslaved Africans, excluded Chinese immigrants in the late 19th century and put Japanese Americans in concentration camps."*

Along the same line, another commentator, Robert Kuttner, sees America as consisting of "two deeply antagonistic cultures each convinced that the other is ruinous."† He likens the conflict to a civil war potentially headed towards a violent one—although the violence is already occurring with mass shootings by civilians, killings by police, vehicle and other attacks on protesters, rubber bullets shot at news reporters and photographers, and intimidation by heavily armed right-wing extremists, all of which have become increasingly a part of the background of daily life.

The violence is disproportionately aimed at non-"whites" and their supporters. Kuttner plausibly states, "The central driver [of civil conflict] is America's founding stain—deep, persistent, brutal racism."‡ Racism, for example, is an undercurrent in the U.S. Supreme Court's

---

* CNN, "There's a sobering truth to Trump's racist tweets that we don't like to admit," July 15, 2019: https://www.cnn.com/2019/07/15/us/trump-tweets-two-americas-blake/index.html
† *American Prospect*, "America's Civil War," June 9, 2020. https://prospect.org/politics/americas-civil-war/
‡ Ibid.

creative interpretation of the Second Amendment* that
gives individuals the right to own weapons to protect
themselves against criminals (viewed generally as
disproportionately "black") and perhaps too against a
government that may someday be controlled by today's
minorities who together are predicted to become a majority
in a few decades.

But if we look beyond the racism, we will see that the
newly interpreted Second Amendment also favors the
wealthy, for it allows the wealthy to own and distribute the
most sophisticated and largest quantity of weaponry
against which a poor man with his treasured rifle has no
chance. Weapons are not just for defense, they are also for
offense, and heavily armed right-wing militia are an
offensive threat to any progress the United States may take
towards greater equality. This threat helps preserve the
status quo.

But while the conflict between the ingrained elite and
those who seek the realization of human equality play out
visibly in societal-wide conflict, the long-term threat to
democracy is not only this visible conflict but also the
heretofore hidden conflict between unconscious acceptance
of ingrained elitism and the goal of realizing the idea of
human equality. This conflict is not only the externally
visible one but also one that has existed hidden throughout
the culture and within every brain. It is not simply a conflict
with the presently existing ingrained elite but with the
societal acceptance of *any* ingrained elite.

The presently existing ingrained elite is also divided, as
many of them are not happy with those who today control
or stifle the government. It may be necessary strategically to

---

* *District of Columbia* v. *Heller*, 554 U.S. 570 (2008). The dangerous
arming of America was a reasonably foreseeable outcome of this
decision.

support the efforts of some members of the ingrained elite in order to depose a current ingrained elite to make it possible for the United States to move forward instead of stagnating or disintegrating into greater violence or chaos. But, if we are to favor human equality, we must not look to some component of the ingrained elite for salvation but see that ingrained elitism itself is what must be increasingly dismantled.

Thus, the existence of two conflicting Americas is both a product of the historical conflict between ingrained elitism and human equality and a distraction from the long-term goal of eliminating ingrained elitism altogether.

What Real Democracy Would Mean

Real democracy—not the societies of today that we call "democracies"—is the social and political setting that incorporates the Extended Golden Rule into daily life. Real democracy requires, among other things, that each person has sufficient resources and opportunity to live a life that is fulfilling. According to an astute observer of Nordic culture and politics, Anu Partanen, government should "make sure that citizens, all citizens, have equal opportunities for well-being—to pursue happiness, enjoy freedom, and achieve success."* This cannot be achieved if some people live in poverty. As long as there is poverty relative to the rest of the population, real democracy has not been achieved.

Real democracy would also require the elimination of racism, sexism and all forms of discrimination against defined groups. It would require equal access for all in choosing their representatives to governing bodies without

---

* *The Nordic Theory of Everything* (New York: HarperCollins, 2016), p. 235.

any advantages given to those with greater wealth. The electoral process would be protected from concentrated corporate and personal wealth.

No nation has yet attained real democracy. Attaining it is a work in progress. It has not been attained, because the Great Chain of Being is a barrier. It will remain a barrier unless we rethink the role of hierarchy in our society, in our culture, and in our personal lives, and alter the role of hierarchies to make them compatible with democracy.

Real democracy also requires recognizing that human equality extends to those who do not believe in human equality. Without this recognition, we would engage in a contradiction that divides the world into those who are equal because they believe in human equality and those who are lesser beings because they do not believe in it. That contradiction would be a denial of human equality in the name of human equality, the same as denial of democracy in the name of democracy.

An example of the absurdity of imposing democracy by force occurred when the United States invaded Iraq in 2003 which then-president George W. Bush ordered—with the initial overwhelming support of the public*—to bring "freedom" to that country. The loss of hundreds of thousands of Iraqi lives was mostly ignored in America, since it was widely assumed that only American deaths were worth counting. This invasion to expand democracy regarded Iraqis not as equal people but as essentially

---

* Polls showed that at the time of the invasion, 72% of the U.S. public approved of the war and around 90% felt that the war was going well. Pewresearch.org, "Public Attitudes Toward the War in Iraq: 2003-2008," by Tom Rosentiel, March 19, 2008. https://www.pewresearch.org/2008/03/19/public-attitudes-toward-the-war-in-iraq-20032008/

irrelevant in the global scheme of things. While maintaining a democracy means protecting it against forces that would destroy it if they are not contained, it cannot mean expanding democracy through war and violence.

President Bush's egregious error, and the error of the public that initially supported him, resulted in a military, economic and humanitarian disaster, but the antecedent error was mental. The anti-democratic disease — ingrained elitism — is a way of thinking, an unconscious ideology that is a force that opposes the idea of human equality. In the Great Chain of Being, Iraqis were not placed as highly as Americans. To combat ingrained elitism, we must recognize its presence and its effect on our social, political and economic structures. If we do not, real democracy will never be fully realized and existing societies called democracies may disintegrate into authoritarian rule or chaos.

But although this disease is a way of thinking, we must not make the mistake of calling this disease *merely* mental. The disease kills people. It supports the lack of community control over police forces, whose members are often allowed to kill and use brutal force disproportionally against ethnic minorities and those who protest these allowances. It underlies the advocacy of war, the sexist treatment of women by men, the racist treatment of people with darker skins, immigration policies based on color and religion, the hierarchical structure of corporations that enables wealth to create more wealth without regard to the welfare of all, the creation and allowance of poverty, the permission given to the wealthy to have greater influence over government and politics, and the policies of the government so influenced that disproportionately benefit the wealthy and, in varying degrees, impoverish the remainder.

The stable existence of these structures with their ingrained elites in turn reinforce mental assumptions that such hierarchy is natural, that some people deserve more power than others. Since the society is structured to give some people more power than others, it can easily be assumed that what is, is what should be. Inequality is embedded in the structure of nearly every facet of life. These structures must be altered to enable the idea of human equality to be fulfilled.

Many Small Steps Required to Move Forward

Usually social change requires many steps, not a sudden leap from the present to the desired future. The United States Constitution, for example, has moved from its undemocratic and pro-slavery beginnings towards a greater degree of democracy through the process of many amendments over many decades. In addition to these amendments, Congressional legislation has been needed to fill in the gaps: the Civil Rights Act of 1964, for example. More amendments and more legislation, local and national, will be needed to continue this progress.

Needed change has also occurred in the form of governmental regulation of the economy, which has grown step by step over many decades. As a result, any imagined line between capitalism and socialism has been blurred. The idea that extensive governmental regulation is necessary for the economy to work is now deeply rooted.

It is, thus, important to give credit to steps in the right direction even though there are many steps left to take. Small steps should not be belittled as not being the whole step, for successful social change generally requires many small, achievable incremental steps, not one gigantic one that rarely happens or, when it does, results in another oppressive hierarchy. There is not one right path to change, but many paths to take and explore.

Some steps, however, are essential if ingrained elitism is to be overcome. One essential step is to transform the role of police. Finding a solution to doing this is simple: Do what Camden, New Jersey did in 2013 and subsequently.* Continued widespread failure to do this or something similar is an unfortunate testament to the enduring strength of the anti-democratic disease.

Altering hierarchical structures also includes transformation of the structure and purpose of corporations, now owned mostly by the wealthy that exist for the openly expressed primary purpose of creating more wealth. Many European nations have taken a small but progressive step by adopting a policy of co-determination ("Mitbestimmung") that requires workers to be represented on corporate boards (currently illegal in the United States).† The long-term goal, however, is to regulate corporations so that their effective purpose is to benefit society as a whole and not just a wealthy elite.

Another example of a partial step in the right direction is in the parts of the sports world that place a cap on teams' wealth or use of wealth, in order to further fairness. Some major sports leagues impose limits on how much each team can spend on its players' salaries. Teams that go over this limit face heavy fines. This places a limit on the ability of a wealthy team to buy the best players and remain dominant. Instead, a team that wins the championship one year may have to shed some of its most expensive players to avoid the fine. Some of the expensive players may have to be redistributed, giving other teams a better chance to enter the top tier and compete for a championship. The team that is the champion one year may come in last the next year. Elite

---

* See "Order above the law," *The Economist*, June 6th, 2020, pp. 17ff.
† *See* "Unseating an old idea" and "What's American for Mitbestimmung," *The Economist*, February 1, 2020, pp. 53-54.

teams are less likely to become ingrained over long periods of time. Transient elitism and hierarchically ranked teams and players are a legitimate and necessary part of sports, but, through league rules that place a cap on team wealth or control its use, *ingrained* elitism is countered and reduced. It is not a perfect process, but it is based on a sound idea and a step in the right direction.

The economy as a whole could work similarly to this part of the sports world by imposing heavy taxes on individual and corporate wealth that exceed a reasonably high threshold. The money collected from the tax could be used to fund benefits for the rest of the population. This would be a partial remedy to the effects of wealth inequality.

Advancing towards real democracy will require additional amending of the United States Constitution to further separate it from its original anti-democratic formulation. The next steps need to be the ratification of the proposed Equal Rights Amendment and the direct election of the president by popular vote without the intervention of the Electoral College. The longer-term goal, and the most essential one, is an amendment that would protect the electoral process from concentrated wealth.

Overall, we must change the existing structures that preserve an ingrained elite, but so that they are not replaced by different structures that are equally anti-democratic.

And a Big Step towards Curing the Anti-Democratic Disease

The anti-democratic disease is a mental and ethical pandemic that infects the world — inside us as well as outside us — and has infected it throughout human history. The vaccine that could protect us from and cure us of this disease is the Extended Golden Rule, as explained above.

The power of the Extended Golden Rule begins with recognition of our inviolate interiority and the realization that others have it too. When this recognition is combined with empathy, we establish the means of emotionally connecting to others. The Golden Rule is the ethical guide for relating to others in a way that is fruitful and respectful. It implicitly contains the idea of our equality to others. But the Golden Rule as traditionally viewed has been limited to our actual interactions with others, and sometimes limited further to bilateral relationships. The transitive rule frees it from these constraints and generates the idea of universal human equality. Human rights enters the picture as the societal and governmental way of coordinating our individualities with others so that the idea of universal equality can be realized in daily life while our individualities are preserved.

While human rights are essential for the protection of this individuality, there are cultural influences lurking in every corner that can get in the way of equality. One critical example of these influences is the tendency of groups to take on a reality of their own that often subordinates the group members to a group identity. This subordination occurs whether group identity is imposed on others by those who assume their own group identity, or is imposed on themselves by members of the group. When this subordination occurs, the members of the group are not viewed primarily as individuals but primarily as components of the group. This is typical of cults, but this practice is much more widespread. The separation of people's identities into "racial," ethnic, national, class, or religious groups provides examples that pervade the entire society.

Although all group identities do not have to function this way, often group identities are locked inside mental gates that encourage the confinement of empathy to within the group and disparage its extension beyond the group. When these identities function this way, they are denials of human equality beyond the group.

Instead of locked gates, the universal equality generated by the Extended Golden Rule unlocks the gates that disconnect us from others, opening us to experiencing others in an empathetic and loving way that inexplicably enhances the enjoyment and meaning of life. These experiences are a fountain of vital energy that injects passion and emotion into the rational formula of equality. This vital energy is not only personally fulfilling, it is also needed to defeat the disease that has prevented real democracy from occurring and to make the societal-wide and cultural changes needed to embody the idea and practice of human equality.

John L. Hodge
July 15, 2020

PART II

THE PRESIDENTS' OWN WORDS

"The idea of 'race' represents one of the most dangerous myths of our time, and one of the most tragic."

—Ashley Montagu, *Man's Most Dangerous Myth: The Fallacy of Race,"* 1942.

"Humans are not divided biologically into distinct continental types or racial genetic clusters."

—Executive Summary of the American Association of Physical Anthropologists' "Statement on Race and Racism" adopted March 27, 2019.

"The legacy of the past racism directed at blacks in the United States is more like a bacillus that we have failed to destroy, a live germ that not only continues to make some of us ill but retains the capacity to generate new strains of a disease for which we have no certain cure."

—George M. Fredrickson, *Racism: A Short History* (2002)

Introduction

Presidents are both products of their culture and powerful proponents of its most salient features. In the United States (and throughout much of the world), racism is deeply embedded in the society and culture. The extent to which U.S. presidents accepted it and promoted it is part of the essential fabric of the nation, a fabric that must be unwoven if democracy is to be fulfilled.

What follows in this Part II are the actual words written, spoken or signed by presidents of the United States since the Civil War. These quoted words speak for themselves and require no explanation beyond my occasional brief commentaries.

Everything added by me in this Part (like this Introduction) is in italics or in footnotes. I state brief overviews of each president labeled as "Comments."

Some presidents are missing. This means that I could not find any statements to quote that clearly indicated a racist viewpoint. This means only that I do not know whether or not they held racist views. I make no inferences from my lack of knowledge. Other researchers may find what I did not. Some things may be newly discovered after the publication of this book, and undoubtedly there are many things I have missed.

I also do not claim to have quoted every racist statement made by the presidents represented here, for I know I have not. I also gave the presidents the benefit of the doubt if statements could be plausibly interpreted differently. Accordingly, I omitted statements that others might view as racist. I have also omitted statements that were potentially "dog-whistles," since understanding them would require analyses that would be beyond the scope of this book.

I have made no attempt to describe or infer anything from the presidents' behaviors or from the words or behaviors of others close to the presidents. What follows is about the presidents' own words, not about their behaviors (except to the extent that words like Executive Orders are also actions) or about inferences that might be made from circumstances. This is not an historical analysis, but simply the words of the presidents themselves.

Andrew Johnson, President
1865 - 1869

Comment: The first U.S. President following the American Civil War of 1861 – 1865, Andrew Johnson was a southerner who opposed citizenship for nonwhites, espoused the inferiority of former slaves, opposed the Fourteenth Amendment, and continued the policies of forcibly relocating indigenous peoples to reservations under the guise of "treaties."

Excerpt from his Veto Message of March 27, 1866 (before the ratification of the Fourteenth Amendment on July 9, 1868 and the Fifteenth Amendment on February 3, 1870): *

"To the Senate of the United States:

"I regret that the bill, which has passed both Houses of Congress, entitled "An act to protect all persons in the United States in their civil rights and furnish the means of their vindication," contains provisions which I can not approve consistently with my sense of duty to the whole

---

* https://www.presidency.ucsb.edu/documents/veto-message-438 . This and similar online references below are to The American Presidency Project of the University of California, Santa Barbara, directed by John Woolley and Gerhard Peters.

people and my obligations to the Constitution of the United States. I am therefore constrained to return it to the Senate, the House in which it originated, with my objections to its becoming a law.

"By the first section of the bill all persons born in the United States and not subject to any foreign power, excluding Indians not taxed, are declared to be citizens of the United States. This provision comprehends the Chinese of the Pacific States, Indians subject to taxation, the people called gypsies, as well as the entire race designated as blacks, people of color. Negroes, mulattoes, and persons of African blood. Every individual of these races born in the United States is by the bill made a citizen of the United States. . . .

"The right of Federal citizenship thus to be conferred on the several excepted races before mentioned is now for the first time proposed to be given by law. If, as is claimed by many, all persons who are native born already are, by virtue of the Constitution, citizens of the United States, the passage of the pending bill can not be necessary to make them such. If, on the other hand, such persons are not citizens, as may be assumed from the proposed legislation to make them such, the grave question presents itself whether, when eleven of the thirty-six States are unrepresented in Congress at the present time, it is sound policy to make our entire colored population and all other excepted classes citizens of the United States. Four millions of them have just emerged from slavery into freedom. Can it be reasonably supposed that they possess the requisite qualifications to entitle them to all the privileges and immunities of citizens of the United States? Have the people of the several States expressed such a conviction? It may also be asked whether it is necessary that they should be declared citizens in order that they may be secured in the enjoyment of the civil rights proposed to be conferred by the bill. Those rights are, by Federal as well as State laws, secured to all domiciled aliens and foreigners, even before the completion of the process of naturalization; and it may safely be assumed that the same enactments are sufficient to give like protection and benefits to those for whom this bill provides special legislation. Besides, the policy of the Government from its origin to the present time seems to have been that persons who are strangers to and unfamiliar with our institutions and our laws should pass through a certain probation, at the end of which, before attaining the coveted prize, they must give evidence of their fitness to receive and to exercise the rights of citizens as contemplated by the Constitution of the United States. The bill in effect proposes a discrimination against large numbers of intelligent, worthy, and patriotic foreigners, and in favor of the Negro, to whom, after long years of bondage, the avenues to freedom and intelligence have just now been suddenly opened. He must of necessity, from his previous unfortunate condition of servitude, be less informed as to the nature and character of our institutions than he who, coming from abroad, has, to some extent at least, familiarized himself with the principles of a Government to which he voluntarily intrusts "life, liberty, and the pursuit of happiness." Yet it is now proposed, by a single legislative enactment, to confer the rights of citizens upon all persons of African descent born within the extended limits of the United States, while persons of foreign birth who make our land their home must undergo a probation of five years, and can only then become citizens upon proof that they are "of good moral character, attached to the principles of the Constitution of the United States, and well disposed to the good order and happiness of the same.

"The first section of the bill also contains an enumeration of the rights to be enjoyed by these classes so made citizens "in every State and Territory in the United States." These rights are "to make and enforce contracts; to sue, be parties, and give evidence: to inherit, purchase, lease, sell, hold, and convey real and personal property," and to have "full and equal benefit of all laws and proceedings for the security of person and property as is enjoyed by white citizens." So, too, they are made subject to the same punishment, pains, and penalties in common with white citizens, and to none other. Thus a perfect equality of the white and colored races is attempted to be fixed by Federal law in every State of the Union over the vast field of State jurisdiction covered by these enumerated rights. In no one of these can any State ever exercise any power of discrimination between the different races. In the exercise of State policy over matters exclusively affecting the people of each State it has frequently been thought expedient to discriminate between the two races. By the statutes of some of the States, Northern as well as Southern, it is enacted, for instance, that no white person shall intermarry with a Negro or mulatto. Chancellor Kent says, speaking of the blacks,

"'Marriages between them and the whites are forbidden in some of the States where slavery does not exist, and they are prohibited in all the slaveholding States; and when not absolutely contrary to law, they are revolting, and regarded as an offense against public decorum.'"

————————

Excerpt from his Veto Message of January 5, 1867: *

"To the Senate of the United States:

"I have received and considered a bill entitled 'An act to regulate the elective franchise in the District of Columbia,' passed by the Senate on the 13th of December and by the House of Representatives on the succeeding day.

. . .

"[I]t is estimated that at the present time there are nearly 100,000 whites to 30,000 Negroes. The cause of the augmented numbers of the latter class needs no explanation. Contiguous to Maryland and Virginia, the District during the war became a place of refuge for those who escaped from servitude, and it is yet the abiding place of a considerable proportion of those who sought within its limits a shelter from bondage. Until then held in slavery and denied all opportunities for mental culture, their first knowledge of the Government was acquired when, by conferring upon them freedom, it became the benefactor of their race. The test of their capability for improvement began when for the first time the career of free industry and the avenues to intelligence were opened to them. Possessing these advantages but a limited time--the greater number perhaps having entered the District of Columbia during the later years of the war, or since its termination--we may well pause to inquire whether, after so brief a probation, they are as a class capable of an intelligent exercise of the right of suffrage and qualified to discharge the duties of official position. The people who are daily witnesses of their mode

---

* https://www.presidency.ucsb.edu/documents/veto-message-422

of living, and who have become familiar with their habits of thought, have expressed the conviction that they are not yet competent to serve as electors, and thus become eligible for office in the local governments under which they live. Clothed with the elective franchise, their numbers, already largely in excess of the demand for labor, would be soon increased by an influx from the adjoining States. Drawn from fields where employment is abundant, they would in vain seek it here, and so add to the embarrassments already experienced from the large class of idle persons congregated in the District. Hardly yet capable of forming correct judgments upon the important questions that often make the issues of a political contest, they could readily be made subservient to the purposes of designing persons. While in Massachusetts, under the census of 1860, the proportion of white to colored males over 20 years of age was 130 to 1, here the black race constitutes nearly one-third of the entire population, whilst the same class surrounds the District on all sides, ready to change their residence at a moment's notice, and with all the facility of a nomadic people, in order to enjoy here, after a short residence, a privilege they find nowhere else. It is within their power in one year to come into the District in such numbers as to have the supreme control of the white race, and to govern them by their own officers and by the exercise of all the municipal authority-- among the rest, of the power of taxation over property in which they have no interest. In Massachusetts, where they have enjoyed the benefits of a thorough educational system. a qualification of intelligence is required, while here suffrage is extended to all without discrimination as well to the most incapable who can prove a residence in the District of one year as to those persons of color who, comparatively few in number, are permanent inhabitants, and, having given evidence of merit and qualification, are recognized as useful and responsible members of the community.

Imposed upon an unwilling people placed by the
Constitution under the exclusive legislation of Congress, it
would be viewed as an arbitrary exercise of power and as
an indication by the country of the purpose of Congress to
compel the acceptance of Negro suffrage by the States. It
would engender a feeling of opposition and hatred between
the two races, which, becoming deep rooted and
ineradicable, would prevent them from living together in a
state of mutual friendliness. Carefully avoiding every
measure that might tend to produce such a result, and
following the clear and well-ascertained popular will, we
should assiduously endeavor to promote kindly relations
between them, and thus, when that popular will leads the
way, prepare for the gradual and harmonious introduction
of this new element into the political power of the country.

. . .

"The exercise of the elective franchise is the highest attribute
of an American citizen, and when guided by virtue,
intelligence, patriotism, and a proper appreciation of our
institutions constitutes the true basis of a democratic form
of government, in which the sovereign power is lodged in
the body of the people. Its influence for good necessarily
depends upon the elevated character and patriotism of the
elector, for if exercised by persons who do not justly
estimate its value and who are indifferent as to its results it
will only serve as a means of placing power in the hands of
the unprincipled and ambitious, and must eventuate in the
complete destruction of that liberty of which it should be
the most powerful conservator. Great danger is therefore to
be apprehended from an untimely extension of the elective
franchise to any new class in our country, especially when
the large majority of that class, in wielding the power thus
placed in their hands, can not be expected correctly to

comprehend the duties and responsibilities which pertain to suffrage. Yesterday, as it were, 4,000,000 persons were held in a condition of slavery that had existed for generations; to-day they are freemen and are assumed by law to be citizens. It can not be presumed, from their previous condition of servitude, that as a class they are as well informed as to the nature of our Government as the intelligent foreigner who makes our land the home of his choice. In the case of the latter neither a residence of five years and the knowledge of our institutions which it gives nor attachment to the principles of the Constitution are the only conditions upon which he can be admitted to citizenship; he must prove in addition a good moral character, and thus give reasonable ground for the belief that he will be faithful to the obligations which he assumes as a citizen of the Republic. Where a people--the source of all political power--speak by their suffrages through the instrumentality of the ballot box, it must be carefully guarded against the control of those who are corrupt in principle and enemies of free institutions, for it can only become to our political and social system a safe conductor of healthy popular sentiment when kept free from demoralizing influences. Controlled through fraud and usurpation by the designing, anarchy and despotism must inevitably follow. In the hands of the patriotic and worthy our Government will be preserved upon the principles of the Constitution inherited from our fathers. It follows, therefore, that in admitting to the ballot box a new class of voters not qualified for the exercise of the elective franchise we weaken our system of government instead of adding to its strength and durability."

Excerpt from his first Veto Message of March 2, 1867: *

"To the House of Representatives:

. . .

"The negroes have not asked for the privilege of voting; the vast majority of them have no idea what it means. This bill not only thrusts it into their bands, but compels them, as well as the whites, to use it in a particular way. If they do not form a constitution with prescribed articles in it and afterwards elect a legislature which will act upon certain measures in a prescribed way, neither blacks nor whites can be relieved from the slavery which the bill imposes upon them. Without pausing here to consider the policy or impolicy of Africanizing the southern part of our territory, I would simply ask the attention of Congress to that manifest, well-known, and universally acknowledged rule of constitutional law which declares that the Federal Government has no jurisdiction, authority, or power to regulate such subjects for any State. To force the right of suffrage out of the hands of the white people and into the hands of the negroes is an arbitrary violation of this principle."

---

* https://www.presidency.ucsb.edu/documents/veto-message-426

Excerpt from his State of the Union Address, December 3, 1867: *

"Fellow-Citizens   of   the   Senate   and   House   of
Representatives:

. . .

"It is manifestly and avowedly the object of these laws to
confer upon Negroes the privilege of voting and to
disfranchise such a number of white citizens as will give the
former a clear majority at all elections in the Southern States.
This, to the minds of some persons, is so important that a
violation of the Constitution is justified as a means of
bringing it about. The morality is always false which
excuses a wrong because it proposes to accomplish a
desirable end. We are not permitted to do evil that good
may come. But in this case the end itself is evil, as well as
the means. The subjugation of the States to Negro
domination would be worse than the military despotism
under which they are now suffering. It was believed
beforehand that the people would endure any amount of
military oppression for any length of time rather than
degrade themselves by subjection to the Negro race.
Therefore they have been left without a choice. Negro
suffrage was established by act of Congress, and the
military officers were commanded to superintend the
process of clothing the Negro race with the political
privileges torn from white men.

---

* https://www.presidency.ucsb.edu/documents/third-annual-message-10

"The blacks in the South are entitled to be well and humanely governed, and to have the protection of just laws for all their rights of person and property. If it were practicable at this time to give them a Government exclusively their own, under which they might manage their own affairs in their own way, it would become a grave question whether we ought to do so, or whether common humanity would not require us to save them from themselves. But under the circumstances this is only a speculative point. It is not proposed merely that they shall govern themselves, but that they shall rule the white race, make and administer State laws, elect Presidents and members of Congress, and shape to a greater or less extent the future destiny of the whole country. Would such a trust and power be safe in such hands?

"The peculiar qualities which should characterize any people who are fit to decide upon the management of public affairs for a great state have seldom been combined. It is the glory of white men to know that they have had these qualities in sufficient measure to build upon this continent a great political fabric and to preserve its stability for more than ninety years, while in every other part of the world all similar experiments have failed. But if anything can be proved by known facts, if all reasoning upon evidence is not abandoned, it must be acknowledged that in the progress of nations Negroes have shown less capacity for government than any other race of people. No independent government of any form has ever been successful in their hands. On the contrary, wherever they have been left to their own devices they have shown a constant tendency to relapse into barbarism. In the Southern States, however, Congress has undertaken to confer upon them the privilege of the ballot. Just released from slavery, it may be doubted whether as a class they know more than their ancestors how to organize and regulate civil society. Indeed, it is admitted that the blacks of the South are not only regardless of the rights of property, but so utterly ignorant of public affairs that their voting can consist in nothing more than carrying a ballot to the place where they are directed to deposit it. I need not remind you that the exercise of the elective franchise is the highest attribute of an American citizen, and that when guided by virtue, intelligence, patriotism, and a proper appreciation of our free institutions it constitutes the true basis of a democratic form of government, in which the sovereign power is lodged in the body of the people. A trust artificially created, not for its own sake, but solely as a means of promoting the general welfare, its influence for good must necessarily depend upon the elevated character and true allegiance of the elector. It ought, therefore, to be reposed in none except those who are fitted morally and mentally to administer it well; for if conferred upon persons who do not justly estimate its value and who are indifferent as to its results, it will only serve as a means of placing power in the hands of the unprincipled and ambitious, and must eventuate in the complete destruction of that liberty of which it should be the most powerful conservator. I have therefore heretofore urged upon your attention the great danger--to be apprehended from an untimely extension of the elective franchise to any new class in our country, especially when the large majority of that class, in wielding the power thus placed in their hands, can not be expected correctly to comprehend the duties and responsibilities which pertain to suffrage. Yesterday, as it were, 4,000,000 persons were held in a condition of slavery that had existed for generations; to-day they are freemen and are assumed by law to be citizens. It can not be presumed, from their previous condition of servitude, that as a class they are as well informed as to the nature of our Government as the intelligent foreigner who makes our land the home of his choice. In the case of the latter neither a residence of five years and the knowledge of our institutions which it gives nor attachment to the principles of the Constitution are the only conditions upon which he can be admitted to citizenship; he must prove in addition a good moral character, and thus give reasonable ground for the belief that he will be faithful to the obligations which he assumes as a citizen of the Republic. Where a people--the source of all political power--speak by their suffrages through the instrumentality of the ballot box, it must be carefully guarded against the control of those who are corrupt in principle and enemies of free institutions, for it can only become to our political and social system a safe conductor of healthy popular sentiment when kept free from demoralizing influences. Controlled through fraud and usurpation by the designing, anarchy and despotism must inevitably follow. In the hands of the patriotic and worthy our Government will be preserved upon the principles of the Constitution inherited from our fathers. It follows, therefore, that in admitting to the ballot box a new class of voters not qualified for the exercise of the elective franchise we weaken our system of government instead of adding to its strength and durability.

"I yield to no one in attachment to that rule of general suffrage which distinguishes our policy as a nation. But there is a limit, wisely observed hitherto, which makes the ballot a privilege and a trust, and which requires of some classes a time suitable for probation and preparation. To give it indiscriminately to a new class, wholly unprepared by previous habits and opportunities to perform the trust which it demands, is to degrade it, and finally to destroy its power, for it may be safely assumed that no political truth is better established than that such indiscriminate and all-embracing extension of popular suffrage must end at last in its destruction. I repeat the expression of my willingness to join in any plan within the scope of our constitutional authority which promises to better the condition of the Negroes in the South, by encouraging them in industry, enlightening their minds, improving their morals, and giving protection to all their just rights as freedmen. But the transfer of our political inheritance to them would, in my opinion, be an abandonment of a duty which we owe alike to the memory of our fathers and the rights of our children.

"The plan of putting the Southern States wholly and the General Government partially into the hands of Negroes is proposed at a time peculiarly unpropitious. The foundations of society have been broken up by civil war. Industry must be reorganized, justice reestablished, public credit maintained, and order brought out of confusion. To accomplish these ends would require all the wisdom and virtue of the great men who formed our institutions originally. I confidently believe that their descendants will be equal to the arduous task before them, but it is worse than madness to expect that Negroes will perform it for us. Certainly we ought not to ask their assistance till we despair of our own competency.

"The great difference between the two races in physical, mental, and moral characteristics will prevent an amalgamation or fusion of them together in one homogeneous mass. If the inferior obtains the ascendency over the other, it will govern with reference only to its own interests for it will recognize no common interest--and create such a tyranny as this continent has never yet witnessed. Already the Negroes are influenced by promises of confiscation and plunder. They are taught to regard as an enemy every white man who has any respect for the rights of his own race. If this continues it must become worse and worse, until all order will be subverted, all industry cease, and the fertile fields of the South grow up into a wilderness. Of all the dangers which our nation has yet encountered, none are equal to those which must result from the success of the effort now making to Africanize the half of our country."

———————————

Excerpt from his Veto Message of June 20, 1868: [*]

"To the House of Representatives:

. . .

"The fifth section of the eighth article provides that "all persons, before registering or voting," must take and subscribe an oath which, among others, contains the following clause:

That I accept the civil and political equality of all men, and agree not to attempt to deprive any person or persons, on account of race, color, or previous condition, of any political or civil right, privilege, or immunity enjoyed by any other class of men.

"It is well known that a very large portion of the electors in all the States, if not a large majority of all of them, do not believe in or accept the political equality of Indians,

———————————

[*] https://www.presidency.ucsb.edu/documents/veto-message-433

Mongolians, or Negroes with the race to which they belong. If the voters in many of the States of the North and West were required to take such an oath as a test of their qualification, there is reason to believe that a majority of them would remain from the polls rather than comply with its degrading conditions."

Excerpt from his State of the Union Address, December 9, 1868: *

"Fellow-Citizens of the Senate and House of Representatives:

. . .

"Treaties with various Indian tribes have been concluded, and will be submitted to the Senate for its constitutional action. I cordially sanction the stipulations which provide for reserving lands for the various tribes, where they may be encouraged to abandon their nomadic habits and engage in agricultural and industrial pursuits. This policy, inaugurated many years since, has met with signal success whenever it has been pursued in good faith and with becoming liberality by the United States. The necessity for extending it as far as practicable in our relations with the aboriginal population is greater now than at any preceding

---

* https://www.presidency.ucsb.edu/documents/fourth-annual-message-9

period. Whilst we furnish subsistence and instruction to the Indians and guarantee the undisturbed enjoyment of their treaty rights, we should habitually insist upon the faithful observance of their agreement to remain within their respective reservations. This is the only mode by which collisions with other tribes and with the whites can be avoided and the safety of our frontier settlements secured."

Ulysses S. Grant, President
1869 - 1877

Comment: General Grant's attack on Jews occurred during the Civil War before he became President. As President, he regarded the indigenous Americans as uncivilized inferiors who had to be channeled into civilization and Christianized (but rather than exterminated). Their reservations had no permanence but receded to make way for newly arrived "white" settlers. The federal government would write and rewrite treaties accordingly to accommodate the settlers, as the reservations' occupants had no bargaining power.

On December 17, 1862, General Grant issued Order No. 11, stating in part: [*]

"The Jews, as a class violating every regulation of trade established by the Treasury Department and also department orders, are hereby expelled from the department within twenty-four hours from the receipt of this order."

---

[*] *The Jewish Virtual Library,* "Anti-Semitism in the United States: General Grant's Infamy," http://www.jewishvirtuallibrary.org/general-grant-s-infamy

[The other "department" refers to The Department of the Tennessee, an administrative district of the Union Army of occupation encompassing Kentucky, Tennessee and Mississippi. A few days later, Grant revoked the order when directed to do so by President Lincoln.]

Excerpt from his State of the Union Address, December 6, 1869: *

"To the Senate and House of Representatives:

. . .

"The building of railroads, and the access thereby given to all the agricultural and mineral regions of the country, is rapidly bringing civilized settlements into contact with all the tribes of Indians. No matter what ought to be the relations between such settlements and the aborigines, the fact is they do not harmonize well, and one or the other has to give way in the end. A system which looks to the extinction of a race is too horrible for a nation to adopt without entailing upon itself the wrath of all Christendom and engendering in the citizen a disregard for human life and the rights of others, dangerous to society. I see no substitute for such a system, except in placing all the Indians on large reservations, as rapidly as it can be done, and giving them absolute protection there."

---

* https://www.presidency.ucsb.edu/documents/first-annual-message-11

———————————

Excerpt from his State of the Union Address, December 5, 1870: *

"To the Senate and House of Representatives:

. . .

"Reform in the management of Indian affairs has received the special attention of the Administration from its inauguration to the present day. The experiment of making it a missionary work was tried with a few agencies given to the denomination of Friends, and has been found to work most advantageously. All agencies and superintendencies not so disposed of were given to officers of the Army. The act of Congress reducing the Army renders army officers ineligible for civil positions. Indian agencies being civil offices, I determined to give all the agencies to such religious denominations as had heretofore established missionaries among the Indians, and perhaps to some other denominations who would undertake the work on the same terms--i.e., as a missionary work. The societies selected are allowed to name their own agents, subject to the approval of the Executive, and are expected to watch over them and aid them as missionaries, to Christianize and civilize the Indian, and to train him in the arts of peace. The Government watches over the official acts of these agents,

———————————

*   https://www.presidency.ucsb.edu/documents/second-annual-message-11

and requires of them as strict an accountability as if they were appointed in any other manner. I entertain the confident hope that the policy now pursued will in a few years bring all the Indians upon reservations, where they will live in houses, and have schoolhouses and churches, and will be pursuing peaceful and self-sustaining avocations, and where they may be visited by the law-abiding white man with the same impunity that he now visits the civilized white settlements."

Excerpts from his statements during an interview as published in **The New York Herald,** *June 8, 1871, p. 5, from an image provided online by Library of Congress, Washington, DC:* *

"Those people . . . who clamor for the destruction of the Indians on the Plans either are interested or know nothing of the condition of affairs in the wild regions where the Indians live. I have lived with the Indians and I know them thoroughly. They can be civilized and made friends of the republic. It takes tact and skill, however, to deal with them. They are shrewd and cunning and won't be shaved out of their rights if they know it. My policy is peace. . . . I want peace on the Plains as everywhere else. . . . That attack on the Apaches was murder, purely. . . . They are warlike — that is, the young savages wander off to rob and murder occasionally; but no doubt they have provocation. I will

---

* https://chroniclingamerica.loc.gov/lccn/sn83030313/1871-06-08/ed-1/seq-5/

investigate the massacre of the Apaches at Camp Grant and be just to all concerned. . . . I don't like riding over and shooting these poor savages; I want to conciliate them and make them peaceful citizens. The policy of peace . . . is much preferable to the policy of war. You can't thrash people so that they will love you, even though they are Indians."

———————————

Excerpt from his State of the Union Address, December 4, 1871: *

"To the Senate and House of Representatives:

. . .

"The policy pursued toward the Indians has resulted favorably, so far as can be judged from the limited time during which it has been in operation. Through the exertions of the various societies of Christians to whom has been intrusted the execution of the policy, and the board of commissioners authorized by the law of April 10, 1869, many tribes of Indians have been induced to settle upon reservations, to cultivate the soil, to perform productive labor of various kinds, and to partially accept civilization. They are being cared for in such a way, it is hoped, as to induce those still pursuing their old habits of life to embrace

———————————

* https://www.presidency.ucsb.edu/documents/third-annual-message-11

the only opportunity which is left them to avoid extermination."

Excerpt from his letter to Maj. Gen. John M. Schofield, March 6, 1872: *

"The anxiety felt by the public generally, and by myself in particular, that Indian hostilities should be avoided in the future, and a policy to civilize and elevate the Indian prove successful, has induced the sending out of a commissioner to study the present condition of Indian affairs in Arizona. . . . Indians who will not put themselves under the restraints required will have to be forced, even to the extent of making war upon them, to submit to measures that will insure security to the white settlers of the Territories. It is not proposed that all the protection shall be to the Indian, but that if they will submit to rules and limitations laid down for them then protection by Military force shall be mutual."

---

* *The Papers of Ulysses S. Grant*, Vol. 23: February 1 – December 31, 1872, v23_066_page 40. https://msstate.contentdm.oclc.org/digital/collection/USG_volume/id/23467

Excerpt from his State of the Union Address, December 1, 1873: *

"To the Senate and House of Representatives:

. . .

"With the encroachment of civilization upon the Indian reservations and hunting grounds, disturbances have taken place between the Indians and whites during the past year, and probably will continue to do so until each race appreciates that the other has rights which must be respected.

"The policy has been to collect the Indians as rapidly as possible on reservations, and as far as practicable within what is known as the Indian Territory, and to teach them the arts of civilization and self-support. Where found off their reservations, and endangering the peace and safety of the whites, they have been punished, and will continue to be for like offenses."

---

* https://www.presidency.ucsb.edu/documents/fifth-annual-message-3

Excerpt from his State of the Union Address, December 7, 1874: *

"To the Senate and House of Representatives:

. . .

"I commend the recommendation of the Secretary for the extension of the homestead laws to the Indians and for some sort of Territorial government for the Indian Territory. A great majority of the Indians occupying this Territory are believed yet to be incapable of maintaining their rights against the more civilized and enlightened white man."

———————

Excerpt from his State of the Union Address, December 5, 1876: †

"To the Senate and House of Representatives:

. . .

"A policy has been adopted toward the Indian tribes inhabiting a large portion of the territory of the United States which has been humane and has substantially ended

* https://www.presidency.ucsb.edu/documents/sixth-annual-message-3
† https://www.presidency.ucsb.edu/documents/eighth-annual-message-3

Indian hostilities in the whole land except in a portion of Nebraska, and Dakota, Wyoming, and Montana Territories — the Black Hills region and approaches thereto. Hostilities there have grown out of the avarice of the white man, who has violated our treaty stipulations in his search for gold. The question might be asked why the Government has not enforced obedience to the terms of the treaty prohibiting the occupation of the Black Hills region by whites. The answer is simple: The first immigrants to the Black Hills were removed by troops, but rumors of rich discoveries of gold took into that region increased numbers. Gold has actually been found in paying quantity, and an effort to remove the miners would only result in the desertion of the bulk of the troops that might be sent there to remove them. All difficulty in this matter has, however, been removed--subject to the approval of Congress--by a treaty ceding the Black Hills and approaches to settlement by citizens."

[The term "citizens" in this passage did not refer to "Indians," who were not citizens and did not become citizens of the United States until June 2, 1924.]

Rutherford B. Hayes, President
1877 - 1881

Comment: President Hayes continued prior policies of confining the indigenous people and introduced new methods to make them conform as much as possible to "white" norms and to impose on them an Anglo-European conception of property. He made disparaging remarks about "Indians," Chinese and "Negroes."

Excerpt from his State of the Union Address, December 2, 1878: *

"Fellow-Citizens of the Senate and House of Representatives:

. . .

"But while the employment of force for the prevention or repression of Indian troubles is of occasional necessity, and wise preparation should be made to that end, greater reliance must be placed on humane and civilizing agencies for the ultimate solution of what is called the Indian problem. It may be very difficult and require much patient

---

* https://www.presidency.ucsb.edu/documents/second-annual-message-12

effort to curb the unruly spirit of the savage Indian to the restraints of civilized life, but experience shows that it is not impossible. Many of the tribes which are now quiet and orderly and self-supporting were once as savage as any that at present roam over the plains or in the mountains of the far West, and were then considered inaccessible to civilizing influences. It may be impossible to raise them fully up to the level of the white population of the United States; but we should not forget that they are the aborigines of the country, and called the soil their own on which our people have grown rich, powerful, and happy. We owe it to them as a moral duty to help them in attaining at least that degree of civilization which they may be able to reach. It is not only our duty, it is also our interest to do so. Indians who have become agriculturists or herdsmen, and feel an interest in property, will thenceforth cease to be a warlike and disturbing element. It is also a well-authenticated fact that Indians are apt to be peaceable and quiet when their children are at school, and I am gratified to know, from the expressions of Indians themselves and from many concurring reports, that there is a steadily increasing desire, even among Indians belonging to comparatively wild tribes, to have their children educated. I invite attention to the reports of the Secretary of the Interior and the Commissioner of Indian Affairs touching the experiment recently inaugurated, in taking fifty Indian children, boys and girls, from different tribes, to the Hampton Normal Agricultural Institute in Virginia, where they are to receive an elementary English education and training in agriculture and other useful works, to be returned to their tribes, after the completed course, as interpreters, instructors, and examples. It is reported that the officer charged with the selection of those children might have had thousands of young Indians sent with him had it been possible to make provision for them. I agree with the Secretary of the Interior in saying that 'the result of this interesting experiment, if favorable, may be destined to become an important factor in the advancement of civilization among the Indians.'"

Excerpt from the Diary and Letters of Rutherford B. Hayes, *February 20, 1879:* *

"I am satisfied the present Chinese labor invasion (It is not in any proper sense immigration. Women and children do not come) is pernicious and should be discouraged. Our experience in dealing with the weaker races—the Negroes and the Indians, for example—is not encouraging. We shall oppress the Chinaman, and their presence will make hoodlums or vagabonds of their oppressors. I therefore would consider with favor suitable measures to discourage the Chinese from coming to our shores."

---

* Charles R. Williams, ed. (Columbus, Ohio: Ohio State Archaeological and Historical Society, 1925-26), III, 522, entry, February 20, 1879; as quoted in George Sinkler, *The Racial Attitudes of American Presidents: From Abraham Lincoln to Theodore Roosevelt* (Garden City, N.Y.: Doubleday, 1971), p. 194.

Excerpt from his State of the Union Address, December 1, 1879: *

"Fellow-Citizens   of   the   Senate   and   House   of Representatives:

. . .

"While these occurrences, in which a comparatively small number of Indians were engaged, are most deplorable, a vast majority of our Indian population have fully justified the expectations of those who believe that by humane and peaceful influences the Indian can be led to abandon the habits of savage life and to develop a capacity for useful and civilized   occupations.   What   they   have   already accomplished in the pursuit of agricultural and mechanical work, the remarkable success which has attended the experiment of employing as freighters a class of Indians hitherto counted among the wildest and most intractable, and the general and urgent desire expressed by them for the education of their children may be taken as sufficient proof that they will be found capable of accomplishing much more if they continue to be wisely and fairly guided. The "Indian policy" sketched in the report of the Secretary of the Interior, the object of which is to make liberal provision for the education of Indian youth, to settle the Indians upon farm lots in severalty, to give them title in fee to their farms, inalienable for a certain number of years, and when their wants are thus provided for to dispose by sale of the lands on their reservations not occupied and used by them, a fund to be formed out of the proceeds for the benefit of the

---

* https://www.presidency.ucsb.edu/documents/third-annual-message-12

Indians, which will gradually relieve the Government of the expenses now provided for by annual appropriations, must commend itself as just and beneficial to the Indians, and as also calculated to remove those obstructions which the existence of large reservations presents to the settlement and development of the country. I therefore earnestly recommend the enactment of a law enabling the Government to give Indians a title in fee, inalienable for twenty-five years, to the farm lands assigned to them by allotment. I also repeat the recommendation made in my first annual message, that a law be passed admitting Indians who can give satisfactory proof of having by their own labor supported their families for a number of years, and who are willing to detach themselves from their tribal relations, to the benefit of the homestead act, and to grant them patents containing the same provision of inalienability for a certain period.

"The experiment of sending a number of Indian children of both sexes to the Hampton Normal and Agricultural Institute, in Virginia, to receive an elementary English education and practical instruction in farming and other useful industries, has led to results so promising that it was thought expedient to turn over the cavalry barracks at Carlisle, in Pennsylvania, to the Interior Department for the establishment of an Indian school on a larger scale. This school has now 158 pupils, selected from various tribes, and is in full operation. Arrangements are also made for the education of a number of Indian boys and girls belonging to tribes on the Pacific Slope in a similar manner, at Forest Grove, in Oregon. These institutions will commend themselves to the liberality of Congress and to the philanthropic munificence of the American people.

"Last spring information was received of the organization of an extensive movement in the Western States, the object of which was the occupation by unauthorized persons of certain lands in the Indian Territory ceded by the Cherokees to the Government for the purpose of settlement by other Indian tribes.

"On the 26th of April I issued a proclamation warning all persons against participation in such an attempt, and by the cooperation of a military force the invasion was promptly checked. It is my purpose to protect the rights of the Indian inhabitants of that Territory to the full extent of the executive power; but it would be unwise to ignore the fact that a territory so large and so fertile, with a population so sparse and with so great a wealth of unused resources, will be found more exposed to the repetition of such attempts as happened this year when the surrounding States are more densely settled and the westward movement of our population looks still more eagerly for fresh lands to occupy. Under such circumstances the difficulty of maintaining the Indian Territory in its present state will greatly increase, and the Indian tribes inhabiting it would do well to prepare for such a contingency. I therefore fully approve of the advice given to them by the Secretary of the Interior on a recent occasion, to divide among themselves in severalty as large a quantity of their lands as they can cultivate; to acquire individual title in fee instead of their present tribal ownership in common, and to consider in what manner the balance of their lands may be disposed of by the Government for their benefit. By adopting such a policy they would more certainly secure for themselves the value of their possessions, and at the same time promote their progress in civilization and prosperity, than by endeavoring to perpetuate the present state of things in the Territory."

Excerpt form a statement made at Johns Hopkins University, October 31, 1890: *

"If there is any young colored man in the South whom we find to have a talent for art or literature, or any special aptitude for study, we are willing to give him money from the education funds to send him to Europe or give him advanced education but hitherto their chief and almost only gift has been that of oratory."

---

* https://www.rbhayes.org/clientuploads/RBHSpeeches/790_-_johns_hopkins_university_-_october_31_1890.htm.   Also partially quoted in George Sinkler, *The Racial Attitudes of American Presidents: from Abraham Lincoln to Theodore Roosevelt* (Garden City, N.Y.: Doubleday, 1971), p. 190.

James A. Garfield, President
1881

Comment: Prior to his short-lived presidency, Garfield voiced the myth of the inferiority of "mixed races."

Excerpt from his speech in the House of Representatives on the Hawaiian Islands, April 6, 1876: *

"In this remark I include the whole group of West India Islands and the whole of the Mexican territory contiguous to the United States. Both these islands and Mexico are inhabited by people of the Latin races strangely degenerated by their mixture with native races. . . . We occupy a portion of that great northern zone which girdles the world, and which has been the theatre of the greatest achievements of civilization, especially in the history of the Anglo-Saxon race. . . ."

---

* Burke A. Hinsdale, *The Works of James A. Garfield* (Boston: James R. Osgood and Co., 1882), Vol II, p. 320

Chester A. Arthur, President
1881 - 1885

Comment: President Arthur, like many before him and many after, expressed views implying that he belongs to a superior civilization.

Excerpt from his State of the Union Address, December 4, 1883: *

"To the Congress of the United States:

. . .

"The provisions for the reciprocal crossing *[by Mexico and the U.S.]* of the frontier by the troops in pursuit of hostile Indians have been prolonged for another year. The operations of the forces of both Governments against these savages have been successful, and several of their most dangerous bands have been captured or dispersed by the skill and valor of United States and Mexican soldiers fighting in a common cause.

---

* https://www.presidency.ucsb.edu/documents/third-annual-message-13

. . .

"Treaty relations with Korea were perfected by the exchange at Seoul, on the 19th of May last, of the ratifications of the lately concluded convention, and envoys from the King of Chosen [Korea] have visited this country and received a cordial welcome. Korea, as yet unacquainted with the methods of Western civilization, now invites the attention of those interested in the advancement of our foreign trade, as it needs the implements and products which the United States are ready to supply. We seek no monopoly of its commerce and no advantages over other nations, but as the Chosenese [Koreans], in reaching for a higher civilization, have confided in this Republic, we can not regard with indifference any encroachment on their rights."

Grover Cleveland, President
1885 - 1889 (First Term)

Comment: President Cleveland called the indigenous people "wards of the government" needing to be civilized under government control. Civilizing them meant Christianizing them and their acceptance of an Anglo-European concept of property. While stating that the purpose of governmental control is to prepare them for citizenship, he also suggested that few if any will become worthy of citizenship.

Excerpt from his State of the Union Address, December 8, 1885: *

"To the Congress of the United States:

. . .

"The most intricate and difficult subject in charge of this Department is the treatment and management of the Indians. I am satisfied that some progress may be noted in their condition as a result of a prudent administration of the present laws and regulations for their control.

---

* https://www.presidency.ucsb.edu/documents/first-annual-message-first-term

"But it is submitted that there is lack of a fixed purpose or policy on this subject, which should be supplied. It is useless to dilate upon the wrongs of the Indians, and as useless to indulge in the heartless belief that because their wrongs are revenged in their own atrocious manner, therefore they should be exterminated.

"They are within the care of our Government, and their rights are, or should be, protected from invasion by the most solemn obligations. They are properly enough called the wards of the Government; and it should be borne in mind that this guardianship involves on our part efforts for the improvement of their condition and the enforcement of their rights. There seems to be general concurrence in the proposition that the ultimate object of their treatment should be their civilization and citizenship. Fitted by these to keep pace in the march of progress with the advanced civilization about them, they will readily assimilate with the mass of our population, assuming the responsibilities and receiving the protection incident to this condition.

"The difficulty appears to be in the selection of the means to be at present employed toward the attainment of this result.

"Our Indian population, exclusive of those in Alaska, is reported as numbering 260,000, nearly all being located on lands set apart for their use and occupation, aggregating over 134,000,000 acres. These lands are included in the boundaries of 171 reservations of different dimensions, scattered in 21 States and Territories, presenting great variations in climate and in the kind and quality of their soils. Among the Indians upon these several reservations there exist the most marked differences in natural traits and disposition and in their progress toward civilization. While some are lazy, vicious, and stupid, others are industrious, peaceful, and intelligent; while a portion of them are self-supporting and independent, and have so far advanced in civilization that they make their own laws, administered through officers of their own choice, and educate their children in schools of their own establishment and maintenance, others still retain, in squalor and dependence, almost the savagery of their natural state.

"In dealing with this question the desires manifested by the Indians should not be ignored. Here again we find a great diversity. With some the tribal relation is cherished with the utmost tenacity, while its hold upon others is considerably relaxed; the love of home is strong with all, and yet there are those whose attachment to a particular locality is by no means unyielding; the ownership of their lands in severalty is much desired by some, while by others, and sometimes among the most civilized, such a distribution would be bitterly opposed.

"The variation of their wants, growing out of and connected with the character of their several locations, should be regarded. Some are upon reservations most fit for grazing, but without flocks or herds; and some on arable land, have no agricultural implements. While some of the reservations are double the size necessary to maintain the number of Indians now upon them, in a few cases, perhaps, they should be enlarged.

"Add to all this the difference in the administration of the agencies. While the same duties are devolved upon all, the disposition of the agents and the manner of their contact with the Indians have much to do with their condition and welfare. The agent who perfunctorily performs his duty and slothfully neglects all opportunity to advance their moral

and physical improvement and fails to inspire them with a
desire for better things will accomplish nothing in the
direction of their civilization, while he who feels the burden
of an important trust and has an interest in his work will, by
consistent example, firm yet considerate treatment, and
well-directed aid and encouragement, constantly lead those
under his charge toward the light of their enfranchisement.
The history of all the progress which has been made in the
civilization of the Indian I think will disclose the fact that
the beginning has been religious teaching, followed by or
accompanying secular education. While the self-sacrificing
and pious men and women who have aided in this good
work by their independent endeavor have for their reward
the beneficent results of their labor and the consciousness of
Christian duty well performed, their valuable services
should be fully acknowledged by all who under the law are
charged with the control and management of our Indian
wards.

. . .

"I recommend the passage of a law authorizing the
appointment of six commissioners, three of whom shall be
detailed from the Army, to be charged with the duty of a
careful inspection from time to time of all the Indians upon
our reservations or subject to the care and control of the
Government, with a view of discovering their exact
condition and needs and determining what steps shall be
taken on behalf of the Government to improve their
situation in the direction of their self-support and complete
civilization; that they ascertain from such inspection what,
if any, of the reservations may be reduced in area, and in
such cases what part not needed for Indian occupation may
be purchased by the Government from the Indians and
disposed of for their benefit; what, if any, Indians may, with

their consent, be removed to other reservations, with a view of their concentration and the sale on their behalf of their abandoned reservations; what Indian lands now held in common should be allotted in severalty; in what manner and to what extent the Indians upon the reservations can be placed under the protection of our laws and subjected to their penalties, and which, if any, Indians should be invested with the right of citizenship."

Excerpt from his State of the Union Address, December 6, 1886: *

"To the Congress of the United States:

. . .

"In September and October last the hostile Apaches who, under the leadership of Geronimo, had for eighteen months been on the war path, and during that time had committed many murders and been the cause of constant terror to the settlers of Arizona, surrendered to General Miles, the military commander who succeeded General Crook in the management and direction of their pursuit.

"Under the terms of their surrender as then reported, and in view of the understanding which these murderous savages seemed to entertain of the assurances given them,

---

* https://www.presidency.ucsb.edu/documents/second-annual-message-first-term

it was considered best to imprison them in such manner as to prevent their ever engaging in such outrages again, instead of trying them for murder. Fort Pickens having been selected as a safe place of confinement, all the adult males were sent thither and will be closely guarded as prisoners. In the meantime the residue of the band, who, though still remaining upon the reservation, were regarded as unsafe and suspected of furnishing aid to those on the war path, had been removed to Fort Marion: The women and larger children of the hostiles were also taken there, and arrangements have been made for putting the children of proper age in Indian schools.

. . .

"The exhibit made of the condition of our Indian population and the progress of the work for their enlightenment, notwithstanding the many embarrassments which hinder the better administration of this important branch of the service, is a gratifying and hopeful one.

. . .

"The present system of agencies, while absolutely necessary and well adapted for the management of our Indian affairs and for the ends in view when it was adopted, is in the present stage of Indian management inadequate, standing alone, for the accomplishment of an object which has become pressing in its importance--the more rapid transition from tribal organizations to citizenship of such portions of the Indians as are capable of civilized life.

"When the existing system was adopted, the Indian race was outside of the limits of organized States and Territories and beyond the immediate reach and operation of civilization, and all efforts were mainly directed to the maintenance of friendly relations and the preservation of peace and quiet on the frontier. All this is now changed. There is no such thing as the Indian frontier. Civilization, with the busy hum of industry and the influences of Christianity, surrounds these people at every point. None of the tribes are outside of the bounds of organized government and society, except that the Territorial system has not been extended over that portion of the country known as the Indian Territory. As a race the Indians are no longer hostile, but may be considered as submissive to the control of the Government. Few of them only are troublesome. Except the fragments of several bands, all are now gathered upon reservations.

"It is no longer possible for them to subsist by the chase and the spontaneous productions of the earth.

"With an abundance of land, if furnished with the means and implements for profitable husbandry, their life of entire dependence upon Government rations from day to day is no longer defensible. Their inclination, long fostered by a defective system of control, is to cling to the habits and customs of their ancestors and struggle with persistence against the change of life which their altered circumstances press upon them. But barbarism and civilization can not live together. It is impossible that such incongruous conditions should coexist on the same soil.

"They are a portion of our people, are under the authority of our Government, and have a peculiar claim upon and are entitled to the fostering care and protection of the nation. The Government can not relieve itself of this responsibility until they are so far trained and civilized as to be able wholly to manage and care for themselves. The paths in which they should walk must be clearly marked out for them, and they must be led or guided until they are familiar with the way and competent to assume the duties and responsibilities of our citizenship.

"Progress in this great work will continue only at the present slow pace and at great expense unless the system and methods of management are improved to meet the changed conditions and urgent demands of the service.

"The agents, having general charge and supervision in many cases of more than 5,000 Indians, scattered over large reservations, and burdened with the details of accountability for funds and supplies, have time to look after the industrial training and improvement of a few Indians only. The many are neglected and remain idle and dependent, conditions not favorable for progress and civilization.

. . .

"Hence the necessity for a supplemental agency or system directed to the end of promoting the general and more rapid transition of the tribes from habits and customs of barbarism to the ways of civilization.

"With an anxious desire to devise some plan of operation by which to secure the welfare of the Indians and to relieve the Treasury as far as possible from the support of an idle and dependent population, I recommended in my previous annual message the passage of a law authorizing the appointment of a commission as an instrumentality auxiliary to those already established for the care of the Indians. It was designed that this commission should be composed of six intelligent and capable persons--three to be detailed from the Army--having practical ideas upon the subject of the treatment of Indians and interested in their welfare, and that it should be charged, under the direction of the Secretary of the Interior, with the management of such matters of detail as can not with the present organization be properly and successfully conducted, and which present different phases, as the Indians themselves differ in their progress, needs, disposition, and capacity for improvement or immediate self-support.

. . .

"There is less opposition to the education and training of the Indian youth, as shown by the increased attendance upon the schools, and there is a yielding tendency for the individual holding of lands. Development and advancement in these directions are essential, and should have every encouragement. As the rising generation are taught the language of civilization and trained in habits of industry they should assume the duties, privileges, and responsibilities of citizenship.

"No obstacle should hinder the location and settlement of any Indian willing to take land in severalty; on the contrary, the inclination to do so should be stimulated at all times when proper and expedient. But there is no authority of law for making allotments on some of the reservations, and on others the allotments provided for are so small that the Indians, though ready and desiring to settle down, are not willing to accept such small areas when their reservations contain ample lands to afford them homesteads of sufficient size to meet their present and future needs.

"These inequalities of existing special laws and treaties should be corrected and some general legislation on the subject should be provided, so that the more progressive members of the different tribes may be settled upon homesteads, and by their example lead others to follow, breaking away from tribal customs and substituting therefor the love of home, the interest of the family, and the rule of the state.

"The Indian character and nature are such that they are not easily led while brooding over unadjusted wrongs. This is especially so regarding their lands. Matters arising from the construction and operation of railroads across some of the reservations, and claims of title and right of occupancy set up by white persons to some of the best land within other reservations require legislation for their final adjustment.

"The settlement of these matters will remove many embarrassments to progress in the work of leading the Indians to the adoption of our institutions and bringing them under the operation, the influence, and the protection of the universal laws of our country."

Excerpt from his State of the Union Address, December 3, 1888: *

"To the Congress of the United States:

----

* https://www.presidency.ucsb.edu/documents/fourth-annual-message-first-term

. . .

"The Apache Indians, whose removal from their reservation in Arizona followed the capture of those of their number who engaged in a bloody and murderous raid during a part of the years 1885 and 1886, are now held as prisoners of war at Mount Vernon Barracks, in the State of Alabama. They numbered on the 31st day of October, the date of the last report, 83 men, 170 women, 70 boys, and 59 girls; in all, 382 persons. The commanding officer states that they are in good health and contented, and that they are kept employed as fully as is possible in the circumstances. The children, as they arrive at a suitable age, are sent to the Indian schools at Carlisle and Hampton.

"Last summer some charitable and kind people asked permission to send two teachers to these Indians for the purpose of instructing the adults as well as such children as should be found there. Such permission was readily granted, accommodations were provided for the teachers, and some portions of the buildings at the barracks were made available for school purposes. The good work contemplated has been commenced, and the teachers engaged are paid by the ladies with whom the plan originated.

"I am not at all in sympathy with those benevolent but injudicious people who are constantly insisting that these Indians should be returned to their reservation. Their removal was an absolute necessity if the lives and property of citizens upon the frontier are to be at all regarded by the Government. Their continued restraint at a distance from the scene of their repeated and cruel murders and outrages is still necessary. It is a mistaken philanthropy, every way injurious, which prompts the desire to see these savages returned to their old haunts. They are in their present location as the result of the best judgment of those having official responsibility in the matter, and who are by no means lacking in kind consideration for the Indians. A number of these prisoners have forfeited their lives to outraged law and humanity. Experience has proved that they are dangerous and can not be trusted. This is true not only of those who on the warpath have heretofore actually been guilty of atrocious murder, but of their kindred and friends, who, while they remained upon their reservation, furnished aid and comfort to those absent with bloody intent.

"These prisoners should be treated kindly and kept in restraint far from the locality of their former reservation; they should be subjected to efforts calculated to lead to their improvement and the softening of their savage and cruel instincts, but their return to their old home should be persistently resisted.

"The Secretary in his report gives a graphic history of these Indians, and recites with painful vividness their bloody deeds and the unhappy failure of the Government to manage them by peaceful means. It will be amazing if a perusal of this history will allow the survival of a desire for the return of these prisoners to their reservation upon sentimental or any other grounds."

Benjamin Harrison, President
1889 - 1893

Comment: President Harrison regarded the Chinese as an "alien" race and continued the prior government's treatment of the indigenous people.

Excerpt from his Letter Accepting the Presidential Nomination, September 11, 1888: *

"We should resolutely refuse to permit foreign governments to send their paupers and criminals to our ports. We are also clearly under a duty to defend our civilization by excluding alien races whose ultimate assimilation with our people is neither possible nor desirable. The family has been the nucleus of our best immigration, and the home the most potent assimilating force in our civilization.

"The objections to Chinese immigration are distinctive and conclusive, and are now so generally accepted as such that the question has passed entirely beyond the stage of argument. The laws relating to this subject would, if I

---

* https://www.presidency.ucsb.edu/documents/letter-accepting-the-presidential-nomination-1

should be charged with their enforcement, be faithfully executed. Such amendments or further legislation as may be necessary and proper to prevent evasions of the laws and to stop further Chinese immigration would also meet my approval. The expression of the convention upon this subject is in entire harmony with my views."

―――――――

Excerpt from his State of the Union Address, December 3, 1889: *

"To the Senate and House of Representatives:

. . .

"Our relations with China have the attentive consideration which their magnitude and interest demand. The failure of the treaty negotiated under the Administration of my predecessor for the further and more complete restriction of Chinese labor immigration, and with it the legislation of the last session of Congress dependent thereon, leaves some questions open which Congress should now approach in that wise and just spirit which should characterize the relations of two great and friendly powers. While our supreme interests demand the exclusion of a laboring element which experience has shown to be incompatible with our social life. . . .

―――――――――――――――

* https://www.presidency.ucsb.edu/documents/first-annual-message-14

. . .

"The report of the Secretary of the Interior exhibits the transactions of the Government with the Indian tribes. Substantial progress has been made in the education of the children of school age and in the allotment of lands to adult Indians. It is to be regretted that the policy of breaking up the tribal relation and of dealing with the Indian as an individual did not appear earlier in our legislation. Large reservations held in common and the maintenance of the authority of the chiefs and headmen have deprived the individual of every incentive to the exercise of thrift, and the annuity has contributed an affirmative impulse toward a state of confirmed pauperism.

"Our treaty stipulations should be observed with fidelity and our legislation should be highly considerate of the best interests of an ignorant and helpless people. The reservations are now generally surrounded by white settlements. We can no longer push the Indian back into the wilderness, and it remains only by every suitable agency to push him upward into the estate of a self-supporting and responsible citizen. For the adult the first step is to locate him upon a farm, and for the child to place him in a school.

"School attendance should be promoted by every moral agency, and those failing should be compelled. The national schools for Indians have been very successful and should be multiplied, and as far as possible should be so organized and conducted as to facilitate the transfer of the schools to the States or Territories in which they are located when the Indians in a neighborhood have accepted citizenship and have become otherwise fitted for such a transfer. This condition of things will be attained slowly, but it will be hastened by keeping it in mind; and in the meantime that cooperation between the Government and the mission schools which has wrought much good should be cordially and impartially maintained.

"The last Congress enacted two distinct laws relating to negotiations with the Sioux Indians of Dakota for a relinquishment of a portion of their lands to the United States and for dividing the remainder into separate reservations. Both were approved on the same day--March 2. The one submitted to the Indians a specific proposition; the other (section 3 of the Indian appropriation act) authorized the President to appoint three commissioners to negotiate with these Indians for the accomplishment of the same general purpose, and required that any agreements made should be submitted to Congress for ratification."

———————

Grover Cleveland, President
1893 - 1897 (Second Term)

Comment: President Cleveland in his second term continued his view that the indigenous people's acceptance of the Anglo-European concept of property is the key to their advancement. After his term of office ended, he spoke of the "negro" in disdainful terms in a way similar to his descriptions of "Indians."

Excerpt from his State of the Union Address, December 4, 1893: *

"To the Congress of the United States:

. . .

"The condition of the Indians and their ultimate fate are subjects which are related to a sacred duty of the Government and which strongly appeal to the sense of justice and the sympathy of our people.

"Our Indians number about 248,000. Most of them are located on 161 reservations, containing 86,116,531 acres of

---

*   https://www.presidency.ucsb.edu/documents/first-annual-message-second-term

land. About 110,000 of these Indians have to a large degree adopted civilized customs. Lands in severalty have been allotted to many of them. Such allotments have been made to 10,000 individuals during the last fiscal year, embracing about 1,000,000 acres. The number of Indian Government schools opened during the year was 195, an increase of 12 over the preceding year. Of this total 170 were on reservations, of which 73 were boarding schools and 97 were day schools. Twenty boarding schools and 5 day schools supported by the Government were not located on reservations. The total number of Indian children enrolled during the year as attendants of all schools was 21,138, an increase of 1,231 over the enrollment for the previous year.

"I am sure that secular education and moral and religious teaching must be important factors in any effort to save the Indian and lead him to civilization. I believe, too, that the relinquishment of tribal relations and the holding of land in severalty may in favorable conditions aid this consummation. It seems to me, however, that allotments of land in severalty ought to be made with great care and circumspection. If hastily done, before the Indian knows its meaning, while yet he has little or no idea of tilling a farm and no conception of thrift, there is great danger that a reservation life in tribal relations may be exchanged for the pauperism of civilization instead of its independence and elevation."

Excerpt from his State of the Union Address, December 3, 1894: *

"To the Congress of the United States:

...

"I have always believed that allotments of reservation lands to Indians in severalty should be made sparingly, or at least slowly, and with the utmost caution. In these days, when white agriculturists and stock raisers of experience and intelligence find their lot a hard one, we ought not to expect Indians, unless far advanced in civilization and habits of industry, to support themselves on the small tracts of land usually allotted to them.

"If the self-supporting scheme by allotment fails, the wretched pauperism of the allottees which results is worse than their original condition of regulated dependence. It is evident that the evil consequences of ill-advised allotment are intensified in cases where the false step can not be retraced on account of the purchase by the Government of reservation lands remaining after allotments are made and the disposition of such remaining lands to settlers or purchasers from the Government.

"I am convinced that the proper solution of the Indian problem and the success of every step taken in that direction depend to a very large extent upon the intelligence and honesty of the reservation agents and the interest they have in their work. An agent fitted for his place can do much toward preparing the Indians under his charge for

---

* https://www.presidency.ucsb.edu/documents/second-annual-message-second-term

citizenship and allotment of their lands, and his advice as to any matter concerning their welfare will not mislead. An unfit agent will make no effort to advance the Indians on his reservation toward civilization or preparation for allotment of lands in severalty, and his opinion as to their condition in this and other regards is heedless and valueless."

————————

Excerpt from his letter to Booker T. Washington, December 3, 1899: *

"It has frequently occurred to me that in the present condition of our free negro population in the South, and the incidents often surrounding them, we cannot absolutely calculate that the future of our nation will be always free from dangers and convulsions, perhaps not less lamentable than those which resulted from the enslaved negroes less than forty years ago. Then the cause of trouble was the injustice of the enslavement of four millions; but now we have to deal with eight millions, who, though free and invested with all the rights of citizenship, still constitute in the body politic a mass largely affected with ignorance, slothfulness, and a resulting lack of appreciation of the obligations of that citizenship.

————————

* As reprinted in *Letters of Grover Cleveland*, ed. Allan Nevins (Boston and New York: Houghton Mifflin Co, 1933), pp. 521-522.

"I am so certain that these conditions cannot be neglected, and so convinced that the mission marked out by the Tuskegee Institute presents the best hope of their amelioration. . . ."

William McKinley, President
1897 - 1901

Comment: President McKinley regarded Filipinos and Chinese as uncivilized races. Like many other presidents, Christianizing others and civilizing them went hand in hand. His views led him to colonize the Philippines.

Excerpt from his State of the Union Address, December 5, 1899: *

"To the Senate and House of Representatives:

. . .

"The future government of the Philippines rests with the Congress of the United States. Few graver responsibilities have ever been confided to us. If we accept them in a spirit worthy of our race and our traditions, a great opportunity comes with them. The islands lie under the shelter of our flag. They are ours by every title of law and equity. They cannot be abandoned. If we desert them we leave them at once to anarchy and finally to barbarism."

---

* https://www.presidency.ucsb.edu/documents/third-annual-message-15

Excerpt from his State of the Union Address, December 3, 1900: *

"The recent troubles in China spring from the antiforeign agitation which for the past three years has gained strength in the northern provinces. Their origin lies deep in the character of the Chinese races and in the traditions of their Government. The Taiping rebellion and the opening of Chinese ports to foreign trade and settlement disturbed alike the homogeneity and the seclusion of China.

"Meanwhile foreign activity made itself felt in all quarters, not alone on the coast, but along the great river arteries and in the remoter districts, carrying new ideas and introducing new associations among a primitive people which had pursued for centuries a national policy of isolation."

---

* https://www.presidency.ucsb.edu/documents/fourth-annual-message-14

Excerpt from 1903 "Interview with President William McKinley" [Referring to colonizing the Philippines after defeating Spain in the war of 1898]: *

"When I next realized that the Philippines had dropped into our laps I confess I did not know what to do with them. I sought counsel from all sides—Democrats as well as Republicans—but got little help. I thought first we would take only Manila; then Luzon; then other islands perhaps also. I walked the floor of the White House night after night until midnight; and I am not ashamed to tell you, gentlemen, that I went down on my knees and prayed Almighty God for light and guidance more than one night. And one night late it came to me this way—I don't know how it was, but it came: (1) That we could not give them back to Spain—that would be cowardly and dishonorable; (2) that we could not turn them over to France and Germany—our commercial rivals in the Orient—that would be bad business and discreditable; (3) that we could not leave them to themselves—they were unfit for self-government—and they would soon have anarchy and misrule over there worse than Spain's was; and (4) that there was nothing left for us to do but to take them all, and to educate the Filipinos, and uplift and civilize and Christianize them, and by God's grace do the very best we could by them, as our fellow-men for whom Christ also died. And then I went to bed, and went to sleep, and slept soundly, and the next morning I sent for the chief engineer

---

* General James Rusling, "Interview with President William McKinley," *The Christian Advocate* 22 January 1903, 17. Reprinted in Daniel Schirmer and Stephen Rosskamm Shalom, eds., *The Philippines Reader* (Boston: South End Press, 1987), 22–23.
http://historymatters.gmu.edu/d/5575/

of the War Department (our map-maker), and I told him to put the Philippines on the map of the United States (pointing to a large map on the wall of his office), and there they are, and there they will stay while I am President!"

Theodore Roosevelt, President
1901 - 1909

Comment: President Theodore Roosevelt was a powerful and influential advocate of white supremacy. His racist pronouncements began before he became president and were included in his popular multi-volume work, The Winning of the West. *His promotion of white supremacy continued during and after his terms of office.*

Excerpts from his "National Life and Character," The Sewanee Review, August, 1894: *

"It is hardly possible to conceive that the peoples of Africa, however ultimately changed, will be anything but negroid in type of body and mind. It is probable that the change will be in the direction of turning them into tribes like those of the Soudan, with a similar religion and morality. It is almost impossible that they will not in the end succeed in throwing off the yoke of the European outsiders, though this end may be, and we hope it will be, many centuries distant.

---

* Reprinted in *The Works of Theodore Roosevelt* (New York: Charles Scribner's Sons, 1926), XIII, pp. 208, 213, 222.

. . .

"From the United States and Australia the Chinaman is kept out because the democracy, with much clearness of vision, has seen that his presence is ruinous to the white race.

"Nineteenth century democracy needs no more complete vindication for its existence that the face that it has kept for the white race the best portions of the new worlds' surface, temperate American and Australia. Had these regions been under aristocratic governments, Chinese immigration would have been encouraged . . . but democracy, with the clear instinct of race selfishness, saw the race foe, and kept out the dangerous alien. The presence of the negro in our Southern States is a legacy from the time when we were ruled by a trans-oceanic aristocracy. The whole civilization of the future owes a debt of gratitude greater than can be expressed in words to that democratic policy which has kept the temperate zones of the new and newest worlds a heritage for the white people.

. . .

"We do not agree with him [Charles H. Pearson] that there is a day approaching when the lower races will predominate in the world and the higher races will have lost their noblest elements. . . . We cannot know beyond peradventure whether we can prevent the higher races from losing their nobler traits and from being overwhelmed by the lower races."

Excerpt from his "Social Evolution," a book review in "The North American Review," July, 1895: *

"A perfectly stupid race can never rise to a very high plane; the negro, for instance, has been kept down as much by lack of intellectual development as by anything else. . . ."

Excerpt from his **The Winning of the West, Part I:** †

"By the time the English had consolidated the Atlantic colonies under their rule, the Indians had become what they have remained ever since, the most formidable savage foes ever encountered by colonists of European stock.

. . .

"The Cherokees were a bright, intelligent race, better fitted to 'follow the white man's road' than any other Indians."

---

* Reprinted in *The Works of Theodore Roosevelt* (New York: Charles Scribner's Sons, 1926), XIII, p. 240.
† (New York: G. P. Putnam's Sons, 1889), pp. 34-35, 80

Excerpt from his State of the Union Address, December 3, 1901: *

"To the Senate and House of Representatives:

. . .

"In the Philippines our problem is larger. They are very rich tropical islands, inhabited by many varying tribes, representing widely different stages of progress toward civilization. Our earnest effort is to help these people upward along the stony and difficult path that leads to self-government. We hope to make our administration of the islands honorable to our Nation by making it of the highest benefit to the Filipinos themselves; and as an earnest of what we intend to do, we point to what we have done. Already a greater measure of material prosperity and of governmental honesty and efficiency has been attained in the Philippines than ever before in their history.

"It is no light task for a nation to achieve the temperamental qualities without which the institutions of free government are but an empty mockery. Our people are now successfully governing themselves, because for more than a thousand years they have been slowly fitting themselves, sometimes consciously, sometimes unconsciously, toward this end. What has taken us thirty generations to achieve, we cannot expect to have another race accomplish out of hand, especially when large portions of that race start very far behind the point which our ancestors had reached even thirty generations ago. In dealing with the Philippine people we must show both patience and

---

* https://www.presidency.ucsb.edu/documents/first-annual-message-16

strength, forbearance and steadfast resolution. Our aim is high. We do not desire to do for the islanders merely what has elsewhere been done for tropic peoples by even the best foreign governments. We hope to do for them what has never before been done for any people of the tropics--to make them fit for self-government after the fashion of the really free nations.

"History may safely be challenged to show a single instance in which a masterful race such as ours, having been forced by the exigencies of war to take possession of an alien land, has behaved to its inhabitants with the disinterested zeal for their progress that our people have shown in the Philippines. To leave the islands at this time would mean that they would fall into a welter of murderous anarchy. Such desertion of duty on our part would be a crime against humanity. The character of Governor Taft and of his associates and subordinates is a proof, if such be needed, of the sincerity of our effort to give the islanders a constantly increasing measure of self-government, exactly as fast as they show themselves fit to exercise it. Since the civil government was established not an appointment has been made in the islands with any reference to considerations of political influence, or to aught else Save the fitness of the man and the needs of the service.

"In our anxiety for the welfare and progress of the Philippines, may be that here and there we have gone too rapidly in giving them local self-government. It is on this side that our error, if any, has been committed. No competent observer, sincerely desirous of finding out the facts and influenced only by a desire for the welfare of the natives, can assert that we have not gone far enough. We have gone to the very verge of safety in hastening the process. To have taken a single step farther or faster in advance would have been folly and weakness, and might well have been crime. We are extremely anxious that the natives shall show the power of governing themselves. We are anxious, first for their sakes, and next, because it relieves us of a great burden. There need not be the slightest fear of our not continuing to give them all the liberty for which they are fit.

"The only fear is test in our overanxiety we give them a degree of independence for which they are unfit, thereby inviting reaction and disaster. As fast as there is any reasonable hope that in a given district the people can govern themselves, self-government has been given in that district. There is not a locality fitted for self-government which has not received it. But it may well be that in certain cases it will have to be withdrawn because the inhabitants show themselves unfit to exercise it; such instances have already occurred. In other words, there is not the slightest chance of our failing to show a sufficiently humanitarian spirit. The danger comes in the opposite direction.

"There are still troubles ahead in the islands. The insurrection has become an affair of local banditti and marauders, who deserve no higher regard than the brigands of portions of the Old World. Encouragement, direct or indirect, to these insurrectors stands on the same footing as encouragement to hostile Indians in the days when we still had Indian wars. Exactly as our aim is to give to the Indian who remains peaceful the fullest and amplest consideration, but to have it understood that we will show no weakness if he goes on the warpath, so we must make it evident, unless we are false to our own traditions and to the demands of civilization and humanity, that while we will do everything in our power for the Filipino who is peaceful, we will take the sternest measures with the Filipino who follows the path of the insurrecto and the ladrone.

"The heartiest praise is due to large numbers of the natives of the islands for their steadfast loyalty. The Macabebes have been conspicuous for their courage and devotion to the flag. I recommend that the Secretary of War be empowered to take some systematic action in the way of aiding those of these men who are crippled in the service and the families of those who are killed.

"The time has come when there should be additional legislation for the Philippines. Nothing better can be done for the islands than to introduce industrial enterprises. Nothing would benefit them so much as throwing them open to industrial development. The connection between idleness and mischief is proverbial, and the opportunity to do remunerative work is one of the surest preventatives of war. Of course no business man will go into the Philippines unless it is to his interest to do so; and it is immensely to the interest of the islands that he should go in. It is therefore necessary that the Congress should pass laws by which the resources of the islands can be developed; so that franchises (for limited terms of years) can be granted to companies doing business in them, and every encouragement be given to the incoming of business men of every kind.

"Not to permit this is to do a wrong to the Philippines. The franchises must be granted and the business permitted only under regulations which will guarantee the islands against any kind of improper exploitation. But the vast natural wealth of the islands must be developed, and the capital willing to develop it must be given the opportunity. The field must be thrown open to individual enterprise, which has been the real factor in the development of every region over which our flag has flown. It is urgently necessary to enact suitable laws dealing with general transportation, mining, banking, currency, homesteads, and the use and ownership of the lands and timber. These laws will give free play to industrial enterprise; and the commercial development which will surely follow will accord to the people of the islands the best proofs of the sincerity of our desire to aid them.

. . .

"Over the entire world, of recent years, wars between the great civilized powers have become less and less frequent. Wars with barbarous or semi-barbarous peoples come in an entirely different category, being merely a most regrettable but necessary international police duty which must be performed for the sake of the welfare of mankind."

Excerpt from his letter to John St. Loe Strachey, September 16, 1904: *

"I do not believe that the average negro in the United States is as yet any way as fit to take care of himself and others as the average white man - for if he were, there would be no negro problem."

---

* Theodore Roosevelt Digital Library, Dickinson State University: http://www.theodorerooseveltcenter.org/Research/Digital-Library/Record?libID=o189210.

————————

Excerpt from his letter to General Grenville Dodge, November 14, 1904: *

"I wish to emphasize that we are not fighting for social equality, and that we do not believe in miscegenation; but that we do believe in equality of opportunity, in equality before the law."

————————

Excerpt from his "Lincoln and the Race Problem," address at the New York City Republican Club, February 13, 1905: †

"If in any community the level of intelligence, morality, and thrift among the colored men can be raised, it is, humanly speaking, sure that the same level among the whites will be raised to an even higher degree. . . .

"The problem is so to adjust the relations between two races of different ethnic type that the rights of neither be abridged

————————

* As quoted in George Sinkler, *The Racial Attitudes of American Presidents: from Abraham Lincoln to Theodore Roosevelt* (Garden City, NY: Doubleday & Co., 1971), p. 331.
† http://www.emersonkent.com/speeches/lincoln_dinner_address.htm

nor jeoparded; that the backward race be trained so that it may enter into the possession of true freedom while the forward race is enabled to preserve unharmed the high civilization wrought out by its forefathers.

. . .

"Laziness and shiftlessness, these, and, above all, vice and criminality of every kind, are evils more potent for harm to the black race than all acts of oppression of white men put together."

————————

Excerpt from his State of the Union Address, December 3, 1906: *

"To the Senate and House of Representatives:

. . .

"The greatest existing cause of lynching is the perpetration, especially by black men, of the hideous crime of rape--the most abominable in all the category of crimes, even worse than murder.

. . .

————————

* https://www.presidency.ucsb.edu/documents/sixth-annual-message-4

"Every colored man should realize that the worst enemy of his race is the negro criminal, and above all the negro criminal who commits the dreadful crime of rape; and it should be felt as in the highest degree an offense against the whole country, and against the colored race in particular, for a colored man to fail to help the officers of the law in hunting down with all possible earnestness and zeal every such infamous offender. Moreover, in my judgment, the crime of rape should always be punished with death. . . .

. . .

"The white man, if he is wise, will decline to allow the Negroes in a mass to grow to manhood and womanhood without education. Unquestionably education such as is obtained in our public schools does not do everything towards making a man a good citizen; but it does much. The lowest and most brutal criminals, those for instance who commit the crime of rape, are in the great majority men who have had either no education or very little; just as they are almost invariably men who own no property; for the man who puts money by out of his earnings, like the man who acquires education, is usually lifted above mere brutal criminality. Of course the best type of education for the colored man, taken as a whole, is such education as is conferred in schools like Hampton and Tuskegee; where the boys and girls, the young men and young women, are trained industrially as well as in the ordinary public school branches."

———————————

Excerpts from his "Biological Analogies in History,"
Romanes lecture for 1910, delivered at Oxford University,
Oxford, England, June 7, 1910: *

"The phenomena of national growth and decay . . . have
been peculiarly in evidence during the four centuries that
have gone by since the discovery of America and the
rounding of the Cape of Good Hope. These have been the
four centuries of by far the most intense and constantly
accelerating rapidity of movement and development that
the world has yet seen. . . . This period of extension and
development has been that of one race, the so-called white
race, or, to speak more accurately, the group of peoples
living in Europe, who undoubtedly have a certain kinship
of blood, who profess the Christian religion, and trace back
their culture to Greece and Rome.

. . .

"No hard-and-fast rule can be drawn as applying to all
alien races, because they differ from one another far more
widely than some of them differ from us. But there are one
or two rules which must not be forgotten. In the long run
there can be no justification for one race managing or
controlling another unless the management and control are
exercised in the interest and for the benefit of that other race.
This is what our peoples have in the main done, and must
continue in the future in even greater degree to do, in India,
Egypt and the Philippines alike. In the next place, as regards
every race, everywhere, at home or abroad, we cannot
afford to deviate from the great rule of righteousness which
bids is treat each man on his worth as a man. He must not

---

* Reprinted in *The Works of Theodore Roosevelt* (New York: Charles
Scribner's Sons, 1926), XII, p. 48, 57-58.

be sentimentally favored because he belongs to a given race; he must not be given immunity in wrong-doing or permitted to cumber the ground, or given other privileges which would be denied to the vicious and unfit among ourselves. On the other hand, where he acts in a way which would entitle him to respect and reward if he was one of our own stock, he is just as entitled to that respect and reward if he comes of another stock, even though that other stock produces a much smaller proportion of men of his type than does our own."

—————————

Excerpt from his "Lynching and the Miscarriage of Justice," **Outlook,** *November 25, 1911:* [*]

"The repeated race riots and lynchings that have occurred in the Northern States during the past decade or so must have convinced the least observant that neither race feeling nor the tendency to lynching is in any sense peculiar to the South. . . . In the many cases in which the lynching is not for rape there is literally not the slightest excuse of any kind or sort that can be advanced for it. . . . Where a man is put to death for rape there need not be the slightest sympathy for him. Such a criminal is outside the pale of humanity. The reason of our condemnation of the crime is not in the slightest degree any sympathy with the malefactor who is slain. . . . We must recognize what the facts are that excite

—————————

[*] Vol. 99, pp. 706-707. http://www.unz.com/print/Outlook-1911nov25-00706/

the mob to act. . . . [A]nd of all crimes the crime of rape is the one which most arouses such furious intensity."

———————

Excerpt from his "The Progressives and the Colored Man," **Outlook, Vol. 101, August 24, 1912, p. 911:** *

"Therefore it is merely the part of wisdom to try our plan, which is to try for the gradual re-enfranchisement of the worthy colored man of the South by frankly giving the leadership of our movement to the wisest and justest white men of the South."

———————

* Vol. 101, p. 911. https://books.google.com/books?id= k4VJAQAAMAAJ&pg=PA909&lpg=PA909&dq= %22progressives+and+the+colored+man%22+ roosevelt&source=bl&ots=FWQW_4-u3t&sig= LaGuqsgeRmRr0GCR3D1Dic2Xw4A&hl=en&sa=X&ved=0ahUK EwjFjMOEkOfZAhWBjlkKHfKLANwQ6AEIMTAC#v=onepage &q=%22progressives%20and%20the%20colored%20man%22%20 roosevelt&f=false

Woodrow Wilson, President
1913 - 1921

Comment: "Woodrow Wilson was in essence a white supremacist" — James Chace, 1912: Wilson, Roosevelt, Taft & Debs — the Election That Changed the Country.*

Excerpt from his article, "The Reconstruction of the Southern States," Atlantic Monthly, January, 1901, p. 1 ff: †

"An extraordinary and very perilous state of affairs had been created in the South by the sudden and absolute emancipation of the Negroes, and it was not strange that the southern legislatures should deem it necessary to take extraordinary steps to guard against the manifest and pressing dangers which it entailed. Here was a vast "laboring, landless, homeless class," once slaves, now free; unpracticed in liberty, unschooled in self-control; never sobered by the discipline of self-support, never established in any habit of prudence; excited by a freedom they did not understand, exalted by false hopes; bewildered and without

---

* (New York: Simon & Schuster, 2004), p. 43.
† As reprinted in *Woodrow Wilson: Essential Writings and Speeches of the Scholar-President*, ed. Mario R. Dinunzio (New York: New York Univ. Press, 2006), pp. 206-207.

leaders, and yet insolent and aggressive; sick of work, covetous of pleasure, a host of dusky children untimely put out of school. . . . They were a danger to themselves as well as to those whom they had once served. . . ."

Excerpts from his statements in **The Public Papers of Woodrow Wilson: College and State:** *

". . . [I]t is our present and immediate task to extend self-government to Porto Rico and the Philippines, if they be fit to receive it,--so soon as they can be made fit.

. . .

"Whether we had a material foothold there or not, it would have been the duty of the United States to play a part, and a leading part at that, in the opening and transformation of the East. . . . The East is to be opened and transformed . . . the standards of the West are to be imposed upon it; nations and peoples which have stood still the centuries through are to be quickened, and make [sic] a part of the universal world of commerce and of ideas which has so steadily been a-making by the advance of European power from age to age. It is our peculiar duty . . . to . . . teach them order and self-control . . . to impart to them . . . the drill

---

* Ed. Ray Stannard Baker and William E. Dodd, Vol 1 (New York: Harper and Brothers, 1925), pp. 410, 412-413, reprinting his article, "Democracy and Efficiency," *Atlantic Monthly*, March, 1901, pp. 289 ff.

and habit of law and obedience which we long ago got out of the strenuous processes of English history. . . . In China, of course, our part will be indirect, but in the Philippines it will be direct. . . .

"This we shall do, not by giving them out of hand our codes of political morality or our methods of political action, the generous gifts of complete individual liberty of the full-fangled institutions of American self-government,--a purple garment for their nakedness,--for these things are not blessings, but a curse, to undeveloped peoples, still in the child of their political growth; but by giving them . . . a government and rule which shall moralize them. . . ."

Excerpts from Woodrow Wilson, **A History of the American People:** *

"*[Referring generally to northerners during Reconstruction]* They had not foreseen that to give the suffrage to the negroes and withhold it from the more capable white men would bestow political power, not upon the negroes, but upon white adventurers, as much the enemies of the one race as of the other.

. . .

"The South, especially, was showing how it could respond to the economic stimulation of the time *[1880s]*, to the

---

* Vol. 5 (New York: Harper & Brothers, 1903), pp. 50, 164, 300, 212.

general development of the resources of the country, now that its corrupt governments, with their negro majorities, were lifted from its shoulders.

. . .

"*[Referring to the end of the nineteenth century and the beginning of the twentieth]* The southern States were readjusting their elective suffrage so as to exclude the illiterate negroes and so in part undo the mischief of reconstruction. . . .

. . .

"*[Referring to the census of 1890]* Throughout the century men of the sturdy stocks of the north of Europe had made up the main strain of foreign blood which was every year added to the vital working force of the country, or else men of the Latin-Gallic stocks of France and northern Italy; but now there came multitudes of men of the lowest class from the south of Italy and men of the meaner sort out of Hungary and Poland, men out of the ranks where there was neither skill nor energy nor any initiative of quick intelligence. . . ."

Excerpt from a memorandum written in 1909 by Woodrow Wilson when he was President of Princeton University: *

"Regret to say that it is altogether inadvisable for a colored man to enter Princeton."

Excerpt from his letter written in 1915 to his second wife: †

"It would be bad enough at best to have anyone we love marry into a Central American family, because there is the presumption that the blood is not unmixed."

---

* John Milton Cooper, Jr., *Woodrow Wilson: A Biography* (New York: Alfred A. Knopf, 2009), p. 109, *citing The Papers of Woodrow Wilson,* ed. Arthur S. Link et al., vol. 18 (Princeton., N.J., 1966-1993), p. 550.
† As quoted in Louis Auchincloss, *Woodrow Wilson* (New York: Penguin Group, 2000), p. 6.

Selections from his Executive Order 2526 — Relating to the Exclusion of Chinese from the Panama Canal Zone, February 6, 1917: *

"By virtue of the authority vested in me by the provisions of the Act of Congress approved August 21, 1916, entitled 'An Act extending certain privileges of Canal employees to other officials on the Canal Zone, and authorizing the President to make rules and regulations affecting the health, sanitation, quarantine, taxation, public roads, self-propelled vehicles and police powers on the Canal Zone, and for other purposes, including provision as to certain fees, money orders and interest deposits', I do hereby establish the following Executive Order for the Canal Zone:

. . .

"Sec. 2. No Chinese person shall be allowed to enter into or remain in the Canal Zone, except as provided in this order; and any Chinese person found in the Canal Zone in contravention of the provisions of this order, shall be punished as hereinafter prescribed.

"Any Chinese person who shall come into the Canal Zone, with the intention of passing into the Republic of Panama, in contravention of the laws of the Republic of Panama, shall be deemed guilty of a violation of this section.

"Sec. 3. The master of any vessel, who shall knowingly bring into the Canal Zone on such vessel and land, or attempt to land, or permit to be landed, any Chinese person, except as

---

* https://www.presidency.ucsb.edu/documents/executive-order-2526-relating-the-exclusion-chinese-from-the-panama-canal-zone

provided for in this order, shall be punished in the manner hereinafter prescribed, for each Chinese person so brought into and landed in the Canal Zone, or attempted or permitted to be landed therein; provided, however, that when a vessel, having Chinese persons on board, comes within the Canal Zone in distress, or under stress of weather, or when a vessel, having Chinese persons on board, touches at a port of the Canal Zone on its voyage to any foreign port or place, such Chinese persons may be permitted to land when authorized by the Governor of The Panama Canal, but they must depart from the Canal Zone with the vessel on its leaving the port.

"Every person who aids or abets in the violation of this order shall be deemed equally guilty with the master of the vessel.

. . .

"Sec. 6. No Chinese member of the crew of any vessel shall be paid off and discharged within sport of the Canal Zone, without the consent of the Panama Canal authorities, unless it be shown by the ship's articles that said Chinese member of the crew signed said articles at a port in the Canal Zone; and seamen or other members of a ship's crew of the Chinese race, when discharged at any port in the Canal Zone under authority of the Governor, may land and remain temporarily therein until a re-shipment is obtained by them, provided a bond in the sum of $500.00 in each case, is executed by such Chinese person, satisfactory to the shipping commissioner, and payable to the Governor of The Panama Canal, and his successors in office, and conditioned that the principal in the bond, in good faith, will obtain a re-shipment and leave the Canal Zone at the earliest date practicable, to be fixed by the shipping commissioner; and said bond may be forfeited, for the full amount thereof, in favor of The Panama Canal, by judgment in the district court of the Canal Zone, should the principal in said bond fail to comply with any of the conditions thereof.

. . .

"Sec. 9. A violation of any of the provisions of this order shall be punished by a fine not to exceed $500.00 or imprisonment not to exceed one year, or both such fine and imprisonment, at the discretion of the court, in conformity with the above mentioned Act of Congress approved August 21, 1916.

"Sec. 10. This order shall take effect sixty (60) days from and after its publication in the Panama Canal Record.

"WOODROW WILSON

"THE WHITE HOUSE

"February 6, 1917."

A statement made by Woodrow Wilson in a meeting attended by Dr. Cary T. Grayson, as quoted in Dr. Grayson's dairy entry of March 5, 1919: *

"[T]he Irish as a race are very hard to deal with owing to their inconsiderateness, their unreasonable demands and their jealousies."

———————

———————

* *The Papers of Woodrow Wilson*, Vol. 55, ed. Arthur S. Link (Princeton: Princeton University Press, 1986), p. 443, as quoted by John Milton Cooper, Jr., *Woodrow Wilson: A Biography* (New York: Alfred A. Knopf, 2009), pp. 481-482, and also by Hans P. Vought, *The Bully Pulpit and the Melting Pot* (Macon, GA: Mercer University Press, 2004), p. 142.

William G. Harding, President
1921-1923

Comment: During his short term prior to his death, President Harding advocated for partial equality for "colored people" but qualified his advocacy with conventional racism.

Excerpt from his "Address of the President of the United States at the Celebration of the Semicentennial Founding of the City of Birmingham, Alabama," October 21, 1921: *

"Politically and economically there need be no occasion for great and permanent differentiation, for limitations of the individual's opportunity, provided that on both sides there shall be recognition of the absolute divergence in things social and racial. When I suggest the possibility of economic equality between the races, I mean it in precisely the same way and to the same extent that I would mean it if I spoke of equality of economic opportunity as between members of the same race. In each case I would mean equality proportioned to the honest capacities and deserts of the individual.

---

* https://voicesofdemocracy.umd.edu/warren-g-harding-address-at-birmingham-speech-text/

"Men of both races may well stand uncompromisingly against every suggestion of social equality. Indeed, it would be helpful to have that word "equality" eliminated from this consideration; to have it accepted on both sides that this is not a question of social equality, but a question of recognizing a fundamental, eternal, and inescapable difference. We shall have made real progress when we develop an attitude in the public and community thought of both races which recognizes this difference.

"Colonizing countries everywhere have in recent times been more and more dealing with the problem from this point of view. The British commonwealth of nations and races confronts it, and has been seeking its solution along the lines here suggested. There is possibility of our learning something applicable to our own country from the British. It is true that there is a great difference between bringing into our own land the colonists of another race and going out to another land and subjecting it and its people to the rule of an alien race. Yet the two cases have so many elements of similarity that it seems to me the experience of each must furnish some light upon the other.

"Take first the political aspect. I would say let the black man vote when he is fit to vote: prohibit the white man voting when he [is] unfit to vote. Especially would I appeal to the self-respect of the colored race. I would inculcate in it the wish to improve itself: distinct race, with a heredity, a set of traditions, an array of aspirations all its own. Out of such racial ambition and pride will come natural segregations, without narrowing any rights, such as are proceeding in both rural and urban communities now in Southern States, satisfying natural inclinations and adding notably to happiness and contentment.

"On the other hand I would insist upon equal educational opportunity for both. This does not mean that both would become equally educated within a generation or two generations or ten generations. Even men of the same race do not accomplish such an equality as that. They never will. The Providence that endowed men with widely unequal capacities and capabilities and energies did not intend any such thing.

"But there must be such education among the colored people as will enable them to develop their own leaders, capable of understanding and sympathizing with such a differentiation between the races as I have suggested— leaders who will inspire the race with proper ideals of race pride, of national pride, of an honorable destiny, an important participation in the universal effort for advancement of humanity as a whole. Racial amalgamation there can not be."

———————————

Calvin Coolidge, President
1923 - 1929

Comment: President Coolidge continued unquestioned his predecessors' doctrine of white supremacy sustained by Christianity.

Excerpt from his article in **Good Housekeeping,** *"Whose Country Is This," February, 1921:* *

"There are racial considerations too grave to be brushed aside for any sentimental reasons. Biological laws tell us that certain divergent people will not mix or blend. The Nordics propagate themselves successfully. With other races, the outcome shows deterioration on both sides. . . .

"From its very beginning our country has been enriched by a complete blend of varied strains in the same ethnic family. . . . That common experience is our history."

---

* Vol. 72, No. 2, p. 13ff. http://hearth.library.cornell.edu/cgi/t/ text/pageviewer-idx?c=hearth;rgn=full%20text;idno=6417403_ 1366_002;view=image;seq=15

Excerpt from his address at Howard University: "The Progress of a People," June 6, 1924: [*]

"It has come to be a legend, and I believe with more foundation of fact than most legends, that Howard University was the outgrowth of the inspiration of a prayer meeting. I hope it is true, and I shall choose to believe it, for it makes of this scene and this occasion a new testimony that prayers are answered. Here has been established a great university, a sort of educational laboratory for the production of intellectual and spiritual leadership among a people whose history, if you will examine it as it deserves, is one of the striking evidences of a soundness of our civilization.

"The accomplishments of the colored people in the United States, in the brief historic period since they were brought here from the restrictions of their native continent, can not but make us realize that there is something essential in our civilization which gives it a special power. I think we shall be able to agree that this particular element is the Christian religion, whose influence always and everywhere has been a force for the illumination and advancement of the peoples who have come under its sway.

"The progress of the colored people on this continent is one of the marvels of modern history. We are perhaps even yet too near to this phenomenon to be able fully to appreciate its significance. That can be impressed on us only as we study and contrast the rapid advancement of the colored people in America with the slow and painful upward

---

[*]   https://www.presidency.ucsb.edu/documents/address-howard-university-the-progress-people

movement of humanity as a whole throughout the long human story.

"An occasion such as this which has brought us here can not but direct our consideration to these things. It has been a painful and difficult experience, this by which an other race has been recruited to the standard of civilization and enlightenment; for that is really what has been going on; and the episodes of Negro slavery in America, of civil war, and emancipation, and, following that, the rapid advancement of the American colored people both materially and spiritually, must be recognized as parts of a long evolution by which all mankind is gradually being led to higher levels, expanding its understanding of its mission here, approaching nearer and nearer to the realization of its full and perfected destiny.

"In such a view of the history of the Negro race in America, we may find the evidences that the black man's probation on this continent was a necessary part in a great plan by which the race was to be saved to the world for a service which we are now able to vision and, even if yet somewhat dimly, to appreciate. The destiny of the great African Continent, to be added at length, and in a future not now far beyond us, to the realms of the highest civilization, has become apparent within a very few decades. But for the strange and long inscrutable purpose which in the ordering of human affairs subjected a part of the black race to the ordeal of slavery, that race might have been assigned to the tragic fate which has befallen many aboriginal peoples when brought into conflict with more advanced communities."

Excerpt from his address accepting the Republican Presidential Nomination, August 14, 1924: *

"Mr. Chairman, Members of the Committee, Ladies and Gentlemen:

. . .

"To preserve American standards for all our inhabitants, whether they were the descendants of former generations residing here or the most recent arrivals, restrictive immigration laws were passed. I should have preferred to continue the policy of Japanese exclusion by some method less likely to offend the sensibilities of the Japanese people. I did what I could to minimize any harm that might arise. But the law has been passed and approved, and the incident is closed. We must seek by some means besides immigration to demonstrate the friendship and respect which we feel for the Japanese nation. Restricted immigration is not an offensive but a purely defensive action. It is not adopted in criticism of others in the slightest degree, but solely for the purpose of protecting ourselves. We cast no aspersions on any race or creed, but we must remember that every object of our institutions of society and Government will fail unless America be kept American."

---

* https://www.presidency.ucsb.edu/documents/address-accepting-the-republican-presidential-nomination-3

Excerpts from his Executive Order 4359-A: *

"Executive Order 4359-A—Citizenship, Passports and Protection
"December 19, 1925

"Article X of the Consular Regulations, 1896, entitled 'Citizens, Passports and Protection,' is hereby canceled and the following substituted:

"ARTICLE X—CITIZENSHIP, PROTECTION, PASSPORTS, AND REGISTRATION. CITIZENSHIP

. . .

"138. CITIZENSHIP BY NATURALIZATION.— Naturalization is a judicial act, and a certificate of naturalization, in regular form, will, in the absence of evidence of fraud in its procurement, be treated by consular officers as conclusive evidence of citizenship, except as herein otherwise provided.

"139. ALIENS WHO MAY NOT BE NATURALIZED.—The existing laws providing for the naturalization of aliens as citizens of the United States apply "to aliens being free white persons, and to aliens of African nativity, and to persons of African descent."—R. S. 2169 AS AMENDED BY THE ACT OF FEBRUARY 18, 1875, 18 STAT. 318. The Supreme Court of the United States has decided that Japanese and Hindus are not free white persons and are not, therefore, capable of

---

*   https://www.presidency.ucsb.edu/documents/executive-order-4359-citizenship-passports-and-protection

naturalization, TAKAO OZAWA VS. UNITED STATES, 260 U. S. 179; IN RE BHAGAT SINGH THIND, 261 U. S. 204. The naturalization of Chinese is specifically prohibited by statute. — SECTION 14, ACT OF MAY 6, 1882, 22 STAT. 58. The naturalization of persons belonging to the above classes is unauthorized and void and consular officers will disregard their certificates of naturalization and will report to the Department concerning their cases. The cases of persons other than Japanese, Chinese and Hindus, whose eligibility to naturalization appears to be doubtful under R. S. 2169 as amended by the Act of February 18, 1875, 18 STAT. 318, should be referred to the Department for decision. In this relation it may be observed that the Supreme Court of the United States has held that persons other than those belonging to the classes specified in R. S. 2169, as amended by the Act of February 18, 1875,18 STAT. 318, such as Japanese, Hindus and Chinese, who served in the armed forces of the United States during the recent World War, are not eligible to citizenship under the seventh subdivision of section 4 of the Act of June 29, 1906, 34 STAT. 601, as amended by the Act of May 9,1918,40 STAT. 542-547, or the Act of July 19, 1919, 41 STAT. 222. — IN RE HIDEMITSU TOYOTA VS. U. S., 45 SUPREME COURT REP. 563.

. . .

"140. NATURALIZATION AND CITIZENSHIP OF MARRIED WOMEN. — It is provided by an Act of Congress of September 22, 1922, 42 STAT. 1021:

. . .

"PROVIDED, That any woman citizen who marries an alien ineligible to citizenship shall cease to be a citizen of the United States.

. . .

[Signed]

"CALVIN COOLIDGE
"THE WHITE HOUSE, *December 19, 1925.*"

Excerpt from his Address before the Union League of Philadelphia, Philadelphia, November 17, 1927:[*]

"Members and Guests of the Union League:

. . .

"I do not mean by America merely that territory stretching from ocean between the Great Lakes and the Rio Grande. That country has lain there throughout the age with its rich plains and mighty forests, its vast deposits of minerals, the far reaches of its watercourses, and all its other natural resources. But, as such, it cast no influence over the lot of humanity. It was only with the coming of the white races of

---

[*]   https://www.presidency.ucsb.edu/documents/address-before-the-union-league-philadelphia-philadelphia-pa

the seventeenth century that it began a career which has
raised it to its present place in the world."

_____

Herbert Hoover, President
1929 - 1933

Comment: President Hoover continued the racist immigration policies of his predecessors. His Proclamation 1872, quoted here, preserved the national ratios of immigrants that had existed before him and continued to treat Asians separately, thereby preserving previous discrimination against them.

Excerpt from his Proclamation 1872, March 22, 1929: *

"Proclamation 1872—Limiting the Immigration of Aliens Into the United States on the Basis of National Origin, March 22, 1929

"By the President of the United States of America

"A Proclamation

"Whereas it is provided in the Act of Congress approved May 26, 1924, entitled 'An Act to limit the immigration of aliens into the United States, and for other purposes,' as

---

* https://www.presidency.ucsb.edu/documents/proclamation-1872-limiting-the-immigration-aliens-into-the-united-states-the-basis

amended by the Joint Resolution of March 4, 1927, entitled 'Joint Resolution to amend subdivisions (b) and (e) of Section 11 of the Immigration Act of 1924, as amended,' and the Joint Resolution of March 31, 1928, entitled 'Joint Resolution to amend subdivisions (b) and (e) of Section 11 of the Immigration Act of 1924, as amended,' that—

" 'The annual quota of any nationality for the fiscal year beginning July 1, 1929, and for each fiscal year thereafter, shall be a number which bears the same ratio to 150,000 as the number of inhabitants in continental United States in 1920 having that national origin (ascertained as hereinafter provided in this section) bears to the number of inhabitants in continental United States in 1920, but the minimum quota of any nationality shall be 100.' Sec. 11(b).

" 'For the purpose of subdivision (b) national origin shall be ascertained by determining as nearly as may be, in respect of each geographical area which under section 12 is to be treated as a separate country (except the geographical areas specified in subdivision (c) of section 4) the number of inhabitants in continental United States in 1920 whose origin by birth or ancestry is attributable to such geographical area. . . .' Sec. 11(c).

" 'For the purpose of subdivisions (b) and (c) the term 'inhabitants in continental United States in 1920' does not include (1) immigrants from the geographical areas specified in subdivision (c) of section 4 or their descendants [generally aliens not subject to quotas], (2) aliens ineligible to citizenship or their descendants [i.e., Asians generally, with specified exceptions]*, (3) the descendants of slave

---

* See A. Warner Parker, "The Ineligible to Citizenship Provisions of the Immigration Act of 1924," The American Journal of International Law, Vol. 19, No. 1 (Jan., 1925), pp. 23-47. This article

immigrants, or (4) the descendants of American aborigines.'
Sec. 11(d)."

. . .

---

examines various interpretations and implementations of complex statutory language that forms much of the basis of this Proclamation.

Franklin D. Roosevelt, President
1933 - 1945

Comment: President Franklin D. Roosevelt expressed anti-Japanese sentiments long before the attack on Pearl Harbor in 1941. His Executive Orders 9066 and 9102, carefully worded to be indirect but the meaning of which is undisputed, authorized the removal of more than 100,000 people with Japanese ancestry, including American citizens, from their homes, including sending them to internment camps and depriving them of their property.

Excerpt from his column, "Roosevelt Says," in **The Macon Daily Telegraph,** *April 30, 1925:* *

. . .

"Let us first examine that nightmare to many Americans, especially our friends in California, the growing population of Japanese on the Pacific slope. It is undoubtedly true that in the past many thousands of Japanese have legally or otherwise got into the United States, settled her and raised

---

* https://georgiainfo.galileo.usg.edu/topics/history/article/
progressive-era-world-war-ii-1901-1945/franklin-d.-roosevelts-
editorials-for-the-macon-telegraph

up children who became American citizens. Californians have properly objected on the sound basic ground that Japanese immigrants are not capable of assimilation into the American population. If this had throughout the discussion been made the sole ground for the American attitude all would have been well, and the people of Japan would today understand and accept our decision.

"Anyone who has traveled in the Far East knows that the mingling of Asiatic blood with European or American blood produces, in nine cases out of ten, the most unfortunate results. There are throughout the East many thousands of so-called Eurasians—men and women and children partly of Asiatic blood and partly of European or American blood. These Eurasians are, as a common thing, looked down on and despised, both by the European and American who reside there, and by the pure Asiatic who lives there.

"The argument works both ways. I know a great many cultivated, highly educated and delightful Japanese. They have all told me that they would feel the same repugnance and objection to having thousands of Americans settle in Japan and intermarry with the Japanese as I would feel in having large numbers of Japanese come over here and intermarry with the American population.

"In this question, then, of Japanese exclusion from the United States, it is necessary only to advance the true reason—the undesirability of mixing the blood of the two peoples. This attitude would be fully understood in Japan, as they would have the same objection to Americans migrating to Japan in large numbers.

. . .

"The Japanese people and the American people are both opposed to intermarriage of the two races — there can be no quarrel there. . . ."

_____

Excerpts from his Executive Order 9066, February 19, 1942: *

"Executive Order 9066 — Authorizing the Secretary of War To Prescribe Military Areas
"February 19, 1942

"WHEREAS the successful prosecution of the war requires every possible protection against espionage and against sabotage to national-defense material, national-defense premises, and national-defense utilities. . . .

"NOW, THEREFORE, by virtue of the authority vested in me as President of the United States, and Commander in Chief of the Army and Navy, I hereby authorize and direct the Secretary of War, and the Military Commanders whom he may from time to time designate, whenever he or any designated Commander deems such actions necessary or desirable, to prescribe military areas in such places and of such extent as he or the appropriate Military Commanders may determine, from which any or all persons may be excluded, and with such respect to which, the right of any person to enter, remain in, or leave shall be subject to

_____

*   https://www.presidency.ucsb.edu/documents/executive-order-9066-authorizing-the-secretary-war-prescribe-military-areas

whatever restrictions the Sectary of War or the appropriate Military Commander may impose in his discretion. The Secretary of War is hereby authorized to provide for residents of any such area who are excluded therefrom, such transportation, food, shelter, and other accommodations as may be necessary, in the judgement of the Secretary of War or the said Military Commander, and until other arrangements are made, to accomplish the purpose of this order. . . .

"I hereby further authorize and direct the Secretary of War and the said Military Commanders to take such other steps as he or the appropriate Military Commander may deem advisable to enforce compliance with the restrictions applicable to each Military area hereinabove authorized to be designated, including the use of Federal troops and other Federal Agencies, with authority to accept assistance of state and local agencies.

"I hereby further authorize and direct all Executive Departments, independent establishments and other Federal Agencies, to assist the Secretary of War or the said Military Commanders in carrying out this Executive Order, including the furnishing of medical aid, hospitalization, food, clothing, transportation, use of land, shelter, and other supplies, equipment, utilities, facilities and services. . . ."

Excerpts from his Executive Order 9102, March 18, 1942: *

"Executive Order 9102 Establishing the War Relocation Authority.
"March 18, 1942

"By virtue of the authority vested in me by the Constitution and statutes of the United States, as President of the United States and Commander in Chief of the Army and Navy, and in order to provide for the removal from designated areas of persons whose removal is necessary in the interests of national security, it is ordered as follows:

"1. There is established in the Office for Emergency Management of the Executive Office of the President the War Relocation Authority, at the head of which shall be a Director appointed by and responsible to the President.

"2. The Director of the War Relocation Authority is authorized and directed to formulate and effectuate a program for the removal, from the areas designated from time to time by the Secretary of War or appropriate military commander under the authority of Executive Order No. 9066 of February 19, 1942, of the persons or classes of persons designated under such Executive Order, and for their relocation, maintenance, and supervision.

"3. In effectuating such program the Director shall have authority to

" — (a) Accomplish all necessary evacuation not undertaken by the Secretary of War or appropriate military commander,

---

*   https://www.presidency.ucsb.edu/documents/executive-order-9102-establishing-the-war-relocation-authority

provide for the relocation of such persons in appropriate places, provide for their needs in such manner as may be appropriate, and supervise their activities.

"(b) Provide, insofar as feasible and desirable, for the employment of such persons at useful work in industry, commerce, agriculture, or public projects, prescribe the terms and conditions of such public employment, and safeguard the public interest in the private employment of such persons.

"(c) Secure the cooperation, assistance, or services of any governmental agency.

"(d) Prescribe regulations necessary or desirable to promote effective execution of such program. . . .

"(e) Make such delegations of authority as he may deem necessary.

"(f) Employ necessary personnel, and make such expenditures, including the making of loans and grants and the purchase of real property, as may be necessary, within the limits of such funds as may be made available to the Authority.

"4. The Director shall consult with the United States Employment Service and other agencies on employment and other problems incident to activities under this Order.

"5. The Director shall cooperate with the Alien Property Custodian appointed pursuant to Executive Order No. 9095 of March 11, 1942, in formulating policies to govern the custody, management, and disposal by the Alien Property Custodian of property belonging to foreign nationals removed under this Order or under Executive Order No. 9066 of February 19, 1942; and may assist all other persons removed under either of such Executive Orders in the management and disposal of their property.

"6. Departments and agencies of the United States are directed to cooperate with and assist the Director in his activities hereunder. The Departments of War and Justice, under the direction of the Secretary of War and the Attorney General, respectively, shall insofar as consistent with the national interest provide such protective, police, and investigational services as the Director shall find necessary in connection with activities under this Order.

"7. There is established within the War Relocation Authority the War Relocation Work Corps. The Director shall provide, by general regulations, for the enlistment in such Corps, for the duration of the present war, of persons removed under this Order or under Executive Order No. 9066 of February 19, 1942, and shall prescribe the terms and conditions of the work to be performed by such Corps, and the compensation to be paid.

"8. There is established within the War Relocation Authority a Liaison Committee on War Relocation, which shall consist of the Secretary of War, the Secretary of the Treasury, the Attorney General, the Secretary of Agriculture, the Secretary of Labor, the Federal Security Administrator, the Director of Civilian Defense, and the Alien Property Custodian, or their deputies, and such' other persons or agencies as the Director may designate. The Liaison Committee shall meet at the call of the Director and shall assist him in his duties.

"9. The Director shall keep the President informed with regard to the progress made in carrying out this Order, and perform such related duties as the President may from time to time assign to him. . . ."

Excerpt from his remarks at the Naval Air Station in Adak, Alaska, August 3, 1944: *

. . .

"No one then visualized the great many thousands of our men in the services who would be up here in Alaska, first throwing the Japs out, and secondly making it impossible for the Japs to come back. Live and learn. That is one thing we are all doing these days. In the days to come I won't trust the Japs around the corner. We have got to make it impossible for them — and we are all doing a great deal to make it impossible for them — to repeat this particular route of access to the United States. That is why it is important, this work we are all doing on this spot. We are going to make it humanly possible to deny access to or aggressive attack by the Japanese of another generation against any part of the United States. . . ."

---

* https://www.presidency.ucsb.edu/documents/remarks-the-naval-air-station-adak-alaska

Harry S. Truman, President
1945 - 1953

Comment: Truman's virulent racism, documented here, preceded his term of office as President though it continued into his terms as a U.S. Senator from 1934 to 1945. As President, he authorized the atomic bombing of Japan. In a remarkable turnaround, he issued Executive Orders to desegregate the Armed Services and sought civil rights legislation that was thwarted by Congress. In 1952 he said, "Talent and genius have no boundaries of race, or nationality, or creed. . . . We should realize that much of the trouble in this world today is the result of false ideas of racial superiority." *

Excerpt from a letter from Harry S. Truman to Bess Wallace, June 22, 1911: †

"I think one man is just as good as another so long as he's

---

* Quote from his Commencement Address at Howard University June 13, 1952. https://www.presidency.ucsb.edu/documents/ commencement-address-howard-university

† https://www.trumanlibrary.gov/library/truman-papers/ correspondence-harry-s-truman-bess-wallace-1910-1919/june-22-1911

honest and decent and not a nigger or a Chinaman. Uncle
Wills says that the Lord made a white man from dust, a
nigger from mud, and then threw what was left and it came
down a Chinaman. He does hate Chinese and Japs. So do I.
It is race prejudice I guess. But I am strongly of the opinion
that negroes ought to be in Arica [sic], yellow men in Asia,
and white men in Europe and America."

———————

*Excerpt from a letter from Harry S. Truman to Bess
Wallace, November 22, 1911:* *

"I was assistant wash lady yesterday. You ought to see me
in that role. Since our nigger woman busted a beer bottle
over her old man's head and ran away, we have had to do
our own washing."

———————

*Excerpt from a letter from Harry S. Truman to Bess
Wallace, March 23, 1912:* †

———————

* https://www.trumanlibrary.gov/library/truman-papers/
correspondence-harry-s-truman-bess-wallace-1910-
1919/november-22-1911
†   https://www.trumanlibrary.gov/library/truman-
papers/

"I suppose the gink who wrote Beautiful Snow has received a genteel sufficiency of it today. I wish he could spend eternity in a big drift. John Greenleaf Whittier, the old nigger lover, also went into spasms over snow. . . ."

———

Excerpt from Letter from Harry S. Truman to Bess Wallace, May 13, 1913: *

"There is the finest copy of Motor out this month. I saw it this morning. It has thoroughly convinced me that I want a Peerless, Lozier, Pierce Arrow, American, Locomobile, Fiat, Marmon, or some other equally cheap car. There are the finest pictures and most convincing ads on those cars you ever saw. I am like the nigger who was asked to change a five-dollar bill when an agent asks me to buy an auto. He said, 'No sir, boss, I can't change it but I thank you sir for the compliment.' If autos were fifty cents each, I wouldn't be able to invest in a hind wheel at present."

———

correspondence-harry-s-truman-bess-wallace-1910-1919/march-23-1912
* https://www.trumanlibrary.gov/library/truman-papers/correspondence-harry-s-truman-bess-wallace-1910-1919/may-13-1913-postmark

Excerpt from Letter from Harry S. Truman to Bess Wallace, June 18, 1913: *

"I remember once when I had to write up an accident on the railroad. A nigger was holding a wheelbarrow straight up by the handles where the fast mail hit him behind and broke his wrist. From the description of it I sent to L. J. Smith he didn't know whether it was the wheelbarrow that had the broken wrist or the fast mail. Neither could he tell if the Santa Fe Missouri Pacific or the boss or the nigger was to blame."

Excerpt from Letter from Harry S. Truman to Bess Wallace, February 4, 1914: †

"I went nigger chasing again on Monday. Right through Central Africa: Vine St. There was no trace of the Nelson nigger."

---

* https://www.trumanlibrary.gov/library/truman-papers /correspondence-harry-s-truman-bess-wallace-1910- 1919/june-18-1913-postmark
† https://www.trumanlibrary.gov/library/truman-papers /correspondence-harry-s-truman-bess-wallace-1910- 1919/february-4-1914-postmark

*Excerpt from Letter from Harry S. Truman to Bess Wallace,
May 12, 1918:* *

"There is absolutely nothing to tell you. I am in the same fix
that Jack Hatfield's nigger was I told you about on the boat.
If you didn't get that letter may be I'd better tell you again.
This coon told Jack he wanted to write to Liza. Jack told him
all right and started the letter for him as Dear Liza. The coon
then said, 'I loves you.' All right Jack told him he had that,
'I loves you.' Jack put that down for him. The coon scratched
his head a while and then said, 'Your lovin' man, Henry.'"

---

*Excerpt from Letter from Harry S. Truman to Margaret
Truman, April 7, 1937:* †

"Dear Margey:-Your dad had dinner last night with the
President and Mrs. Roosevelt. . . . They gave a real good
meal at the taxpayers expense - tomato soup, fillet of
flounder, roast turkey, string beans, pineapple salad,
chocolate ice cream and cake, candy and little caf? noir
afterwards. All these things were in courses, deftly placed
and removed by an army of coons. I suggested to Mrs.

---

* https://www.trumanlibrary.gov/library/truman-papers/
correspondence-harry-s-truman-bess-wallace-1910-
1919/may-12-1918
† https://www.trumanlibrary.gov/library/truman-papers/
correspondence-harry-s-truman-margaret-truman-1927-
1964/april-7-1937

Minton on that these negros were evidently the top of the black social set in Washington."

———————

Excerpt from Letter from Harry S. Truman to Bess W. Truman, July 31, 1939: *

"I went up to the Metropolitan by myself and saw Man about Town. It is a very funny show. The nigger steals the screen."

———————

Excerpt from Letter from Harry S. Truman to Bess W. Truman, August 4, 1939: †

"Well this is nigger picnic day."

———————

* https://www.trumanlibrary.gov/library/truman-papers/correspondence-harry-s-truman-bess-wallace-truman-1921-1959/july-31-1939
† https://www.trumanlibrary.gov/library/truman-papers/correspondence-harry-s-truman-bess-wallace-truman-1921-1959/august-4-1939

Excerpt from Letter from Harry S. Truman to Bess W. Truman, September 15, 1940: *

"My desk is a mess, just killed a cockroach. He walked right out on the arm rest where I'm writing this as impudently as a sassy nigger."

———————————

———————————

* https://www.trumanlibrary.gov/library/truman-papers/ correspondence-harry-s-truman-bess-wallace-truman-1921- 1959/september-15-0

Dwight D. Eisenhower, President
1953-1961

Comment: President Eisenhower may have made no clearly racist statements in public or in writing, but his racist sentiments were captured in oral statements to reliable sources as quoted here. Eisenhower's view of Brown v. Board of Education* *(the U.S. Supreme Court's 1954 decision holding that segregated "separate but equal" schools were unconstitutional), as reported below by Arthur Larson (who held high positions in the Eisenhower administrations and wrote a biography of him), is consistent with the absence of any public statement by Eisenhower agreeing with the decision, but he did enforce it against southern obstruction.*

President Eisenhower's statement about segregationist southerners made to Earl Warren, then Chief Justice of the U. S. Supreme Court, during the Court's consideration of Brown v. Board of Education *(1954):* †

"These are not bad people. All they are concerned about is to see that their sweet little girls are not required to sit in school alongside some big overgrown Negroes."

---

* 347 U.S. 483 (1954)

† Chief Justice Earl Warren, *The Memoirs of Earl Warren* (Garden City, New York: Doubleday & Co., 1977), p. 291.

Report by Arthur Larson stating that President Eisenhower commented on July 26, 1956, about overcoming racial discrimination: *

"*[Overcoming racial discrimination does not mean]* that a Negro should court my daughter."

Statement by President Eisenhower on October 1, 1957, made to and reported by Arthur Larson, of his view of the United States Supreme Court decision in **Brown** *v.* **Board of Education:** †

"I personally think the decision was wrong."

---

* Arthur Larson, *Eisenhower: The President Nobody Knew* (New York: Charles Scribner's Sons, 1968), p. 127.
† Larson, *Eisenhower: The President Nobody Knew*, p. 124.

Richard M. Nixon, President
1969 - 1974

Comment: President Nixon was an anti-Semite who, in private conversations, confided with others who he believed shared his views. He regarded "blacks" and Mexicans as inferior to "whites." Curiously, he recorded his private conversations that are now available to the public. (Below, the taped conversations are grouped together.)

Quoted excerpt from President Nixon's memorandum to John Ehrlichman, Jauuary 28, 1972: *

"THE WHITE HOUSE
"WASHINGTON
"January 28, 1972
"MEMORANDUM FOR JOHN EHRLICHMAN
"FROM THE PRESIDENT

"Copy for Bob Haldeman no   distribution   beyond   those two

---

* https://www.nixonlibrary.gov/sites/default/files/ virtuallibrary/documents/jan10/032.pdf

"Since reading Ed Morgan's memorandum on the Richmond School Case, I have been doing a lot of thinking about the whole problem of integrated education and integrated housing.

. . .

"I am convinced that while legal segregation is totally wrong that forced integration of housing or education is just as wrong.

"I realize that this position will lead us to a situation in which blacks will continue to live for the most part in black neighborhoods and where there will be predominatly [sic] black schools and predominatly white schools in the metropolitan areas. While I cannot go as far as Scammon in contending that' those who insist on forced integrated education are really practicing white supremacy there is unfortunately a grain of truth in it. Brown vs, Board of Education in effect held that legally segregated education was inferior education. Once the legal barriers which caused segregation were removed and the segregation continued the philosophy of Brown would be that any segregated education, whether it was because of law or because of fact, is inferior. That is why I see the courts eventually reaching the conclusion that de facto segregation must also be made legally unacceptable. But if we rip away all the hypocrisy of the extreme supporters of the Brown philosophy, we have to conclude that it is only segregated black education which is inferior and that actually segregated white education is probably superior to education in which there is too great a degree of integration of inferior black students with the white students. I realize that I am going counter against' all the social arguments that a child's experience is greatly increased by being exposed to black children as well as white children when he is going to school. I am totally for that. I went to schools where we had some Black children, Mexican children and others in grade school, high school and in college. But at least they were children who were in the same school with a reasonable chance to do about as well as their white colleagues. They were not so hopelessly far behind that they dragged the others down with them. Again, let me say that I am aware of Coleman's and Moynihan's thesis that slow learners do not hold back fast learners, etc., but I simply don't agree with it, particularly when we add the extra ingredient of mixing Black and White teachers on a pro-rated basis.

. . .

"Even if I should become convinced--and I don't think it would be possible to convince me--that forced integration of education and housing was in the best interests of Blacks and not too detrimental to Whites I could not possibly support it in good conscience. What I am saying through this memorandum is that as a matter of conscience I have reached a conclusion, motivated not by politics but by my considered evaluation of all the issues involved, that I must speak to these two controversial issues now firmly, without equivocation, and if necessary through the advocacy of a constitutional amendment. . . ."

Excerpts from President Nixon's statements recorded in The
White House Tapes: *

"I have look the greatest affection for blacks, but I know
they're not going to make it for five hundred years. They
aren't. You know that too. Mexicans, a different cup of tea,
their heritage. At the present time, they steal, they're
dishonest. But they do have a concept of family life with it
so they don't live like a bunch of dogs the way Negroes do
live. . . ."
  --From the meeting of President Nixon, Chief of Staff H. R.
  ("Bob") Haldeman, and John D. Ehrlichman, May 13, 1971.

"I want to look at any sensitive areas around where Jews are
involved. . . . Jews are all through the government. . . . We've
got to get a man in charge who is not Jewish to control the
Jewish. . . . The government is full of Jews. . . . Most Jews are
disloyal. . . . Generally speaking, Bob, you can't trust the
bastards. They turn on you. . . . They have this arrogant
attitude. . . ."
  --From the meeting of President Nixon and Chief of Staff H.
  R. ("Bob") Haldeman, July 3, 1971.

---

* Derived from these sources: Harry Shearer, "Nixon's the One,"
YouTube videos, Episodes 1, 3 and 4, reenactments quoting the
tapes, beginning at https://www.youtube.com/watch?v=
YEQFt3mO2-I; John Prados, ed., *The White House Tapes* (New
York: The New Press, 2003) (includes CDs that reproduce some of
the tapes), pp. 243-245, 247-248; John A. Farrell, *Richard Nixon*
(New York: Doubleday, 2017), pp. 385-386, 426. Some portions of
the tapes are unintelligible.

"The Jews are born spies. . . . They are just in it up to their necks."

   --From the meeting of President Nixon and Chief of Staff H. R. ("Bob") Haldeman, July 5, 1971.

"Would you please get the names of the Jews . . . big Jewish contributors of the Democrats. . . . Could we please investigate some of these cocksuckers? . . ."

   --From the meeting of President Nixon and Chief of Staff H. R. ("Bob") Haldeman, September 13, 1971.

"It's a very interesting thing, they're all Jews, you can't talk about it in public with them. . . . Needless to say . . . generational . . . , a level of politics all . . . by Jews. . . . In the media now, money, it's totally dominated by Jews. Newsweek is totally, is all by Jewish and dominated by their editorial pages. The New York Times, The Washington Post, totally Jewish. . . . The owners of The Los Angeles Times. . . . The other thing, you know, is that all three networks except for, say, they have top men . . . may not be of that persuasion. But the writers going, ninety-five percent are Jewish. Now, what does that mean? Does this mean that, uh, that all of Jews are bad and all, but it does mean that all Jews are left wing, way particularly the younger ones like that. They're way out, they're radical, they're peace at any price except where . . . is concerned. . . . The only thing that you could tell me would be that . . . the Middle East. The best Jews actually are the Israeli Jews. . . . Because Israel, the reason is Meir supports me. . . . She knows that a Democrat will give you the communists, the Russians. She doesn't want it. . . . Russian Jew, boy the, does she know that? . . .

Barney Laske, . . . and Max Fisher, . . . Pat Macauther . . . .
But . . . insists that the difficulty is it, that not only are they
Jews, but, but boy they take care of each other. Now every
group has a tendency to that. Catholic tends to hire a
Catholic, and . . . Quaker perhaps tries to, wants to hire a
Quaker. But the Jews. . . . Boy, they . . . hire Jews. . . . The
media in this country is extremely dangerous. . . . When we
get back in, we'll take care of it."
  *--From the meeting of President Nixon, Reverend Billy
  Graham, Chief of Staff H. R. ("Bob") Haldeman, and Press
  Secretary Ronald L. Ziegler, February 1, 1972.*

"Take Vietnam. . . . The North Vietnamese would have
probably slaughtered, castrated, two million South
Vietnamese Catholics. And, I know I shouldn't care, these
little brown people so far away, as you know very well as
you say. But on the other hand, we couldn't do that, not
because of Vietnam, but because of Japan, because of
Germany, because of the Middle East. . . ."
  *--From the meeting of President Nixon, Reverend Billy
  Graham, Chief of Staff H. R. ("Bob") Haldeman, and Press
  Secretary Ronald L. Ziegler, February 1, 1972.*

Ronald Reagan, President
1981 - 1989

Comment: President Ronald Reagan expressed racist views about African nations prior to his presidency.

Statement made by Reagan when Governor of California in a phone call made to President Nixon on October 26, 1971, tape-recorded by Nixon: *

"Those monkeys from those African countries—damn them—they're still uncomfortable wearing shoes."

---

*https://www.soundcloud.com/user-10784335/reagan-nixon-call; also quoted in online article in the *Atlantic*, "Ronald Reagan's Long-Hidden Racist Conversation with Richard Nixon," by Tim Naftali, July 30, 2019, https://www.theatlantic.com/ideas/archive/2019/07/ronald-reagans-racist-conversation-richard-nixon/595102/

Donald Trump, President
2017 - *

Comment: The racist statements of President Trump preceded his presidency and continued after he became president. As explained below, he treats Muslims as though they were a race. His anti-Muslim statements are listed separately.

Excerpt from his statement made to an interviewer in 2014.†

"I'm proud to have that German blood."

---

* This book was published a few months before the November 3, 2020 presidential election.
† The quote is documented in a video of Donald Trump speaking: https://www.youtube.com/watch?v=gvVFd6J_MA8 (dated January 21, 2017); also, https://www.youtube.com/watch?v=_Nj6fUaf49Y; the exact date and place of the quote, reportedly made in 2014, seems not to be known. The quote also appears elsewhere, for example in: History News Network, "Trump's Bad "Bloodlines," by Rafael Medoff, June, 7, 2020: http://hnn.us/article/175833

Excerpt from his Presidential Announcement Speech, June 16, 2015: *

"When Mexico sends its people, they're not sending their best. They're not sending you. They're not sending you. They're sending people that have lots of problems, and they're bringing those problems with us. They're bringing drugs. They're bringing crime. They're rapists. And some, I assume, are good people."

Excerpt from his interview with CNN "Pressroom" on June 3, 2016: †

"I've been treated very unfairly by this judge. Now, this judge is of Mexican heritage. I'm building a wall, OK? . . . This judge is giving us unfair rulings. Now I say why? Well, I want to — I'm building a wall, OK, and it's a wall between Mexico, not another country."

---

* *Time*, "Here's Donald Trump's Presidential Announcement Speech," June 16, 2015: http://time.com/3923128/donald-trump-announcement-speech/
† *CNN*, "Tapper to Trump '...is that not the definition of racism?'" June 3, 2016: http://cnnpressroom.blogs.cnn.com/2016/06/03/tapper-to-trump-is-that-not-the-definition-of-racism/

Excerpt from his statements during the debate with presidential candidate Hillary Clinton on September 26, 2016: *

"We have a situation where we have our inner cities, African-Americans, Hispanics are living in hell because it's so dangerous. You walk down the street, you get shot."

Excerpt from his statements during the third debate with presidential candidate Hillary Clinton, October 20, 2016: †

"Our inner cities are a disaster. You get shot walking to the store. They have no education. They have no jobs."

---

* *NPR,* "Fact Check: Trump And Clinton Debate For The First Time," September 26, 2016: https://www.npr.org/2016/09/26/495115346/fact-check-first-presidential-debate?utm_source=twitter.com&utm_medium=social&utm_campaign=npr&utm_term=nprnews&utm_content=20160926?utm_source=twitter.com&utm_medium=social&utm_campaign=npr&utm_term=nprnews&utm_content=20160926 ; also https://www.washingtonpost.com/news/the-fix/wp/2016/09/26/the-first-trump-clinton-presidential-debate-transcript-annotated/?utm_term=.65389ec68935
† *Politico,* "Full transcript: Third 2016 presidential debate," October 20, 2016: https://www.politico.com/story/2016/10/full-transcript-third-2016-presidential-debate-230063

Statement he made at a meeting in the Oval Office, January 18, 2018, referring to African countries, El Savador and Haiti: *

"Why are we having all these people from shithole countries come here?"

———————

Another statement he made at a meeting in the Oval Office, January 18, 2018: †

"We should have more people from Norway."

———————

* *Washington Post,* "Trump derides protections for immigrants from 'shithole' countries, " by Josh Dawsey, January 12, 2018: https://www.washingtonpost.com/politics/trump-attacks-protections-for-immigrants-from-shithole-countries-in-oval-office-meeting/2018/01/11/bfc0725c-f711-11e7-91af-31ac729add94_story.html?utm_term=.0ebfc4f7552c ; *Boston Globe,* "Senator Durbin, who was in the room with Trump, says president said 'racist' things," by Jill Colvin and Alan Fram: http://www.bostonglobe.com/news/politics/2018/01/12/senator-durbin-who-was-room-with-trump-says-president-said-racist-things/unrlwYfCsrQg7ezE9W3KtJ/story.html
† Reuters, "'Thanks, but no thanks' - Norwegians reject Trump's immigration offer," by Terje Solsvik and Camilla Knudsen, January 12, 2018, https://www.reuters.com/article/us-usa-trump-immigration-norway/thanks-but-no-thanks-norwegians-reject-trumps-immigration-offer-idUSKBN1F11QK

Another statement he made at a meeting in the Oval Office, January 18, 2018: *

"Why do we need more Haitians? Take them out."

Comment: Following are three of his comments concerning "African-Americans" which are notable for containing language with "racial" innuendo, attributing to them lack of intelligence or calling them lower or animalistic life forms.

Excerpt from his "tweet" at 1:11 PM, June 25, 2018: †

---

* *Washington Post,* "'Shithole' wasn't the most offensive part of Trump's Haiti comments," January 12, 2018.
https://www.washingtonpost.com/opinions/shithole-wasnt-the-most-offensive-part-of-trumps-haiti-comments/2018/01/12/beba1ea6-f7b3-11e7-a9e3-ab18ce41436a_story.html?hpid=hp_no-name_opinion-card-f%3Ahomepage%2Fstory&utm_term=.1d6943a36c84
† https://twitter.com/realDonaldTrump/status/1011295779422695424

"Congresswoman Maxine Waters, an extraordinarily low IQ person, has become, together with Nancy Pelosi, the Face of the Democrat Party."

———————

Excerpt from his "tweet" at 11:37 PM, August 3, 2018: *

"Lebron James was just interviewed by the dumbest man on television, Don Lemon. He made Lebron look smart, which isn't easy to do."

———————

Excerpt from his "tweet" at 7:31 AM, August 14, 2018, referring to former White House staffer Omarosa Manigault-Newman: †

———————

* *Deadline*, "Donald Trump Manages To Insult Both Don Lemon and LeBron James In Single Tweet," by Nellie Andreeva, August 3, 2018. https://deadline.com/2018/08/donald-trump-manages-to-insult-both-don-lemon-and-lebron-james-in-single-tweet-1202440125/

† *Washington Post*, "Trump's response to Omarosa continues a pattern some find concerning," by Eugene Scott, August 14, 2018. https://www.washingtonpost.com/politics/2018/08/14/trumps-response-omarosa-continues-pattern-some-find-concerning/

"When you give a crazed, crying lowlife a break, and give her a job at the White House, I guess it just didn't work out. Good work by General Kelly for quickly firing that dog!"

---

*Content of three "tweets" he made on July 14, 2019, concerning four members of the U.S. House of Representatives who are not "white," three of whom were born in the United States: ***

"So interesting to see 'progressive' Democrat congresswomen, who originally came from countries whose governments are a complete and total catastrophe, the worst, most corrupt and inept anywhere in the world (if they even have a functioning government at all), now loudly and viciously telling the people of the United States, the greatest and most powerful nation on earth, how our government is to be run. Why don't they go back and help fix the totally broken and crime-infested places from which they came. Then come back and show us how it is done."

---

* https://twitter.com/realDonaldTrump/status/
1150381394234941448 ; BBC, "Trump's tweet: What did he say and why's he being criticised?" July 18, 2019;
https://www.bbc.co.uk/newsround/49004860

Excerpt from his "tweets" of July 27, 2019, beginning at 7:14 AM, referring to an "African American" congressman and the district he represents: *

"Rep. Elijah Cummings has been a brutal bully, shouting and screaming at the great men & women of Border Patrol about conditions at the Southern Border, when actually his Baltimore district is FAR WORSE and more dangerous. His district is considered the Worst in the USA.

"As proven last week during a Congressional tour, the border is clean, efficient & well run, just very crowded. Cumming (sic) district is a disgusting, rat- and rodent-infested mess. If he spent more time in Baltimore, maybe he could help clean up this very dangerous & filthy place.

"Why is so much money sent to the Elijah Cummings' district when it is considered the worst run and most dangerous anywhere in the United States? No human being would want to live there."

---

* WBALTV, "President Trump slams Cummings, calls Baltimore 'disgusting, rat- and rodent-infested mess,'" July 27, 2019. https://www.wbaltv.com/article/president-donald-trump-tweet-rep-elijah-cummings-baltimore/28526792

Excerpt from his "tweets" of July 1, 2020, 9:48 AM: *

"NYC is cutting Police $'s by ONE BILLION DOLLARS, and yet the @NYCMayor is going to paint a big, expensive, yellow Black Lives Matter sign on Fifth Avenue, denigrating this luxury Avenue. . . . Maybe our GREAT Police, who have been neutralized and scorned by a mayor who hates & disrespects them, won't let this symbol of hate be affixed to New York's greatest street. Spend this money fighting crime instead!"

––––––––––––––––––

––––––––––––––––––

* NPR, "Trump: Painting 'Black Lives Matter' On 5th Avenue Would Be 'Symbol Of Hate,'" by Barbara Sprunt and Kelsey Snell, July 1, 2020. https://www.npr.org/sections/live-updates-protests-for-racial-justice/2020/07/01/885944289/trump-painting-black-lives-matter-on-5th-avenue-would-be-symbol-of-hate

Comment: Following, grouped together, are many of Trump's statements referring to Muslims. It is not a complete list. *Although Muslims are not a "race," many Americans view them as people who are not "white," so that racism factors into religious prejudice against Islam. Donald Trump's statements against Muslims attack them for their innate group behavior, thus imbuing them with racial characteristics. Accordingly, his expressed negative views of Muslims are appropriately viewed as a form of racism, just as anti-Semitism is a form of racism. This would be obvious in Trump's statements if we replaced "Muslims" with, say, "Jews" or "blacks."*

Excerpt from a radio interview of Trump on March 30, 2011, referring to then President Obama: †

"He doesn't have a birth certificate, or if he does, there's something on that certificate that is very bad for him. Now, somebody told me — and I have no idea if this is bad for him or not, but perhaps it would be — that where it says 'religion,' it might have 'Muslim.' And if you're a Muslim, you don't change your religion, by the way."

---

* See, for example, Medium.com, "86 Times Donald Trump Displayed or Promoted Islamophobia," April 19, 2018, a list compiled using data gathered by Georgetown University's Bridge Initiative. https://medium.com/nilc/86-times-donald-trump-displayed-or-promoted-islamophobia-49e67584ac10
† https://www.youtube.com/watch?v=WqaS9OCoTZs

Three connected statements by Trump: the first stated by Trump at a rally in Birmingham, Alabama on November 21, 2015, the second by Trump on ABC News on November 22, 2015, and the third an exchange between Trump and George Stephanopoulos on ABC's "This Week," on November 22, 2015. No evidence has emerged supporting Trump's statements: [*]

"Hey, I watched when the World Trade Center came tumbling down. And I watched in Jersey City, New Jersey, where thousands and thousands of people were cheering as that building was coming down. Thousands of people were cheering."

"If you look at for instance where I said the thousands of Muslims were cheering. It turned out to be true."

---

[*] Politifact, "Fact-checking Trump's claim that thousands in New Jersey cheered when World Trade Center tumbled," by Lauren Carroll, November 22, 2015: https://www.politifact.com/factchecks/2015/nov/22/donald-trump/fact-checking-trumps-claim-thousands-new-jersey-ch/ ; ABC News, "What ABC News Footage Shows of 9/11 Celebrations," by Imtiyaz Delawala, December 4, 2015: https://abcnews.go.com/Politics/abc-news-footage-shows-911-celebrations/story?id=35534125 ; *Washington Post*, "Trump's outrageous claim that 'thousands' of New Jersey Muslims celebrated the 9/11 attacks," by Glenn Kessler, November 22, 2015: https://www.washingtonpost.com/news/fact-checker/wp/2015/11/22/donald-trumps-outrageous-claim-that-thousands-of-new-jersey-muslims-celebrated-the-911-attacks/

"There were people that were cheering on the other side of New Jersey, where you have large Arab populations. They were cheering as the World Trade Center came down. I know it might be not politically correct for you to talk about it, but there were people cheering as that building came down — as those buildings came down. And that tells you something. It was well covered at the time, George. Now, I know they don't like to talk about it, but it was well covered at the time. There were people over in New Jersey that were watching it, a heavy Arab population, that were cheering as the buildings came down. Not good."

———————

Excerpt from CBS News, "Face the Nation transcripts December 6, 2015: Trump, Christie, Sanders": [*]

"DICKERSON: Have people been too politically correct with Muslims in America?

"TRUMP: I think so. I think so, and with maybe other things, too, but I think certainly so.

"And, as you know, I came out with, I want vigilance, I want real vigilance, and whether it's mosques or whatever it has to be, but a lot of bad things are happening.

———————

[*] https://www.cbsnews.com/news/face-the-nation-transcripts-december-6-2015-trump-christie-sanders/

"DICKERSON: Whatever it has to be, does that include -- I know you -- where are you on the question of tracking Muslims in America?

"TRUMP: Well, look, we are having a problem with radical -- with radicals in the Muslim group. Let's not kid ourselves.

"And you can say it or you don't have to say it. And maybe you won't even want to, but I have been saying it loud and strong. So, if you have people coming out of mosques with hatred and with death in their eyes and on their minds, we're going to have to do something, John.

"We can't just say, we're not going to look at it. Now, I made that statement a number of weeks ago. It took a lot of -- a lot of whatever. A lot of people were not exactly thrilled with it. And now everybody seems to agree with me.

"DICKERSON: But this idea of tracking Muslims in America, that's the thing. Where are you on that? . . .

"TRUMP: You have people that have to be tracked. If they're Muslims, they're Muslims. But you have people that have to be tracked.

"And we better be -- I use the word vigilance. We have to show vigilance. We have to have it. And if we don't, we're foolish people. . . .

"DICKERSON: There are three million Muslims in America.

"TRUMP: Right.

"DICKERSON: What should they feel about their place in American life now?

"TRUMP: Look, we are having a tremendous problem with radical Islamic terrorism. And you can say it, or you don't have to say it.

"And we have a president that won't issue the term. He won't talk about it. So, we're having this tremendous radical Islamic terrorism. OK? A lot of people don't want to even say it. Not a lot of people. We have one person that I really know of, and it's called President Obama.

"Until he admits that this is a problem, we're never going to solve the problem. But he's only going to be there, fortunately, a little bit more than a year, because the problem will get solved when he gets the hell out.

"DICKERSON: You mentioned political correctness about Muslims. What the criticism of you is, that you are playing on fears that people have and that you're stoking...

"TRUMP: No, I'm playing on common sense.

"No, no, I'm not playing on fears. I don't want to play on fears. I understand the whole world. And I -- I understand. And I have Muslim friends who are great people. And, by the way, they tell me there's a big problem.

"I'm not playing on fears. I'm playing on common sense. We have a problem. The World Trade Center came down. And, by the way, speaking of coming down, they put their families on airplanes a couple of days before, sent them back to Saudi Arabia, for the most part.

"Those wives knew exactly what was going to happen. And those wives went home to watch their husbands knock down the World Trade Center, the Pentagon, and wherever the third plane was going, except we had some very, very brave passengers, wherever that third plane was going.

"DICKERSON: You mentioned the families, going after the families. What does that -- what does that mean? How would it work?

"TRUMP: Well, I would go after -- well, at least I would certainly go after the wives who absolutely knew what was happening.

"And I guess your definition of what I would do, I'm going to leave that to your imagination. But I will tell you I would be very tough on families, because the families know what is happening.

"Even in this last instance, I see everybody knew. So many people knew. They thought that this man and this woman, whether he was radicalized or how he became, they thought something was going on. Why don't these people report it to the police? Why wouldn't they report it to the police?

"Now, they said it was profiling. They didn't want to profile.

"Can you believe this? They didn't want to profile, even though they thought something very bad was going on.

"DICKERSON: But his sister said she didn't know what was going on. She was crestfallen for the victims here.

"TRUMP: I probably don't believe the sister.

"DICKERSON: You don't believe the sister.

"TRUMP: No."

———————

Statement read by Trump at a rally in Mount Pleasant, South Carolina, on December 7, 2015. The statement had been issued earlier that day by Trump's campaign: *

"'Donald J. Trump is calling for a total and complete shutdown of Muslims entering the United States until our country's representatives can figure out what is going on.'"

———————

Excerpt from Trump's responses during an interview by Anderson Cooper on March 9, 2016: †

"I think Islam hates us. There's something there that — there's a tremendous hatred there. There's a tremendous

———————

* *Washington Post*, "Trump calls for 'total and complete shutdown of Muslims entering the United States,'" by Jenna Johnson, December 7, 2015. https://www.washingtonpost.com/news/post-politics/wp/2015/12/07/donald-trump-calls-for-total-and-complete-shutdown-of-muslims-entering-the-united-states/
† CBSNews, "Donald Trump: "I think Islam hates us," by Reena Flores, March 10, 2016. https://www.cbsnews.com/news/donald-trump-i-think-islam-hates-us/

hatred. We have to get to the bottom of it. There's an unbelievable hatred of us."

———————

Excerpts from his statements on Fox Business Network, March 22, 2016: *

"We're having problems with the Muslims, and we're having problems with Muslims coming into the country. . . You need surveillance. You have to deal with the mosques, whether you like it or not. These attacks . . . are not done by Swedish people."

———————

* Medium.com, "86 Times Donald Trump Displayed or Promoted Islamophobia," April 19, 2018. https://medium.com/nilc/86-times-donald-trump-displayed-or-promoted-islamophobia-49e67584ac10. Also, https://www.washingtonpost.com/news/post-politics/wp/2017/05/20/i-think-islam-hates-us-a-timeline-of-trumps-comments-about-islam-and-muslims/

Excerpt from an interview with Trump on March 29, 2016: *

"[ANDERSON] COOPER: And welcome back. We're coming to you tonight from the Riverside Theater in downtown Milwaukee with the "360" townhall. The three remaining Republican candidates campaigning hard with the primary here just a week away. We heard so far from Senator Ted Cruz. Right now the GOP front-runner, New York businessman Donald Trump.

. . .

"COOPER: The other, though, part of Lieutenant Murphy's question was about protecting the rights of minority groups, of Muslims, or Sikhs, of Jews, and others inside the United States...

"TRUMP: ... I want to do that also, and I do want to do that, but I at the same time we have to recognize we have a serious problem.

"COOPER: Let me follow up on that. You said you agreed, I think you said you agreed, with Senator Ted Cruz's proposal in the wake of the Brussels attack that law enforcement should, quote, "patrol and secure Muslim neighborhoods before they become radicalized." I talked to him about this in the last hour.

---

* CNN, "Full Rush Transcript: Donald Trump, CNN Milwaukee Republican Presidential Town Hall," March 29th, 2016.
https://cnnpressroom.blogs.cnn.com/2016/03/29/full-rush-transcript-donald-trump-cnn-milwaukee-republican-presidential-town-hall/

"Bill Bratton, Commissioner, the Chief of Police...

"TRUMP: ... Who I like very much...

"COOPER: ... In your home city. Chief of Police under Giuliani, as well as now de Blasio, again — out in L.A. He said about Ted Cruz's proposal, "we do not patrol and secure neighborhoods based on selective enforcement because of race or religion." Is he wrong?

"TRUMP: I think we have to be extremely vigilant in those areas, we have to look very seriously at the Mosques. Lots of things happening in the Mosques, that's been proven. You look at what's going on in Paris where Mosques are being closed, OK? And, we have to look very, very seriously.

"COOPER: There's a lot of Muslims in America who hear that, saying we got to look seriously at the Mosques...

"TRUMP: ... Let me just tell you something, in San Bernadino people know what was going on. These two people — probably became radicalized through her. Who knows? Frankly, right now, it doesn't matter.

"But, these two people want to kill their co-workers, et cetera, et cetera, in their apartment, or their house. In their place where they lived, they had bombs all over the apartment...

"COOPER: ... Do you trust...

"TRUMP: ... Excuse me — they had bombs on the floor. Many people saw this. Many, many people. Muslims living with them in the same area. They saw that house, they saw that.

"One didn't want to turn them in. He said I don't know turn them in because I don't want to be accused of racial profiling. He saw bombs all over the apartment, OK?

"It's just an excuse...
"COOPER: ... Do you trust Muslims in America?

"TRUMP: ... Do I what?

"COOPER: Trust Muslims in America?

"TRUMP: Many of them I do. Many of them I do, and some, I guess, we don't. Some, I guess, we don't. We have a problem, and we can try and be very politically correct and pretend we don't have a problem, but, Anderson, we have a major, major problem. This is, in a sense, this is a war...

"COOPER: ... So, special patrols in Muslim neighborhoods...

"TRUMP: ... You know, nobody wants to call it a war — excuse me. Nobody wants to call it a war. It's a war. There's a war."

———————————

Excerpt from an interview with Trump that was broadcast on Fox News "Fox and Friends" on May 20, 2016 in response to a statement that banning Muslims supports terrorism: *

"… if anything it's just the opposite … they're going to have to turn in the people that are bombing the planes. And they know who the people are. And we're not going to find the people by just continuing to be so nice and so soft. . . ."

———————

Excerpt from Trump's speech at a rally in Greensboro, North Carolina on June 14, 2016: †

"So the killer's parents immigrated from Afghanistan as the Washington Times reported the children of Muslim American parents, they're responsible for a growing number for whatever reason a growing number of terrorist attacks."

———————

———————————————

* https://www.youtube.com/watch?v=388ZzbaPlYc (at approximately 5:46 into the video).

† ABCNews, "Donald Trump: Number of Muslim Immigrants Have 'Hostile Attitudes.' " by Candace Smith and John Santucci, June 14, 2016. https://abcnews.go.com/Politics/donald-trump-number-muslim-immigrants-hostile-attitudes/story?id=39844183

Excerpt from an interview on NBC's "Meet the Press," July 24, 2016: *

"CHUCK TODD:
"On whether he's backing off on his Muslim band.

"DONALD TRUMP:
"I actually don't think it's a pull-back. In fact, you could say it's an expansion."

———————————

Excerpt from his speech given in Youngstown, Ohio, August 15, 2016: †

"The time is overdue to develop a new screening test. . . . I call it extreme vetting. . . . We must also screen out . . . who believe that Sharia law should supplant American law."

———————————

* https://www.nbcnews.com/meet-the-press/meet-press-july-24-2016-n615706

† Video excerpt of Trump speech: CNN, "Donald Trump wants 'extreme vetting' of immigrants. What is the US doing now?" by Lauren Said-Moorhouse and Ryan Browne, August 16, 2015. https://www.cnn.com/2016/08/16/politics/how-us-vets-immigrants-donald-trump-extreme-vetting/. Also, CNN, "What is Sharia law?" by Gul Tuysuz, August 16, 2015. https://www.cnn.com/2016/08/16/world/sharia-law-definition/index.html

---

[These quotations of President Trump ended on July 1, 2020.]

APPENDIX

UNITED NATIONS:
Universal Declaration of Human Rights

Preamble

Whereas recognition of the inherent dignity and of the
equal and inalienable rights of all members of the human
family is the foundation of freedom, justice and peace in
the world,

Whereas disregard and contempt for human rights have
resulted in barbarous acts which have outraged the
conscience of mankind, and the advent of a world in which
human beings shall enjoy freedom of speech and belief
and freedom from fear and want has been proclaimed as
the highest aspiration of the common people,

Whereas it is essential, if man is not to be compelled to
have recourse, as a last resort, to rebellion against tyranny
and oppression, that human rights should be protected by
the rule of law,

Whereas it is essential to promote the development of
friendly relations between nations,

Whereas the peoples of the United Nations have in the
Charter reaffirmed their faith in fundamental human

rights, in the dignity and worth of the human person and in the equal rights of men and women and have determined to promote social progress and better standards of life in larger freedom,

Whereas Member States have pledged themselves to achieve, in co-operation with the United Nations, the promotion of universal respect for and observance of human rights and fundamental freedoms,

Whereas a common understanding of these rights and freedoms is of the greatest importance for the full realization of this pledge,

Now, Therefore THE GENERAL ASSEMBLY proclaims THIS UNIVERSAL DECLARATION OF HUMAN RIGHTS as a common standard of achievement for all peoples and all nations, to the end that every individual and every organ of society, keeping this Declaration constantly in mind, shall strive by teaching and education to promote respect for these rights and freedoms and by progressive measures, national and international, to secure their universal and effective recognition and observance, both among the peoples of Member States themselves and among the peoples of territories under their jurisdiction.

Article 1.

All human beings are born free and equal in dignity and rights. They are endowed with reason and conscience and should act towards one another in a spirit of brotherhood.

Article 2.

Everyone is entitled to all the rights and freedoms set forth in this Declaration, without distinction of any kind, such as race, colour, sex, language, religion, political or other opinion, national or social origin, property, birth or other status. Furthermore, no distinction shall be made on the basis of the political, jurisdictional or international status of the country or territory to which a person belongs, whether it be independent, trust, non-self-governing or under any other limitation of sovereignty.

Article 3.

Everyone has the right to life, liberty and security of person.

Article 4.

No one shall be held in slavery or servitude; slavery and the slave trade shall be prohibited in all their forms.

Article 5.

No one shall be subjected to torture or to cruel, inhuman or degrading treatment or punishment.

Article 6.

Everyone has the right to recognition everywhere as a person before the law.

Article 7.

All are equal before the law and are entitled without any discrimination to equal protection of the law. All are entitled to equal protection against any discrimination in violation of this Declaration and against any incitement to such discrimination.

Article 8.

Everyone has the right to an effective remedy by the competent national tribunals for acts violating the fundamental rights granted him by the constitution or by law.

Article 9.

No one shall be subjected to arbitrary arrest, detention or exile.

Article 10.

Everyone is entitled in full equality to a fair and public hearing by an independent and impartial tribunal, in the determination of his rights and obligations and of any criminal charge against him.

Article 11.

(1) Everyone charged with a penal offence has the right to be presumed innocent until proved guilty according to law in a public trial at which he has had all the guarantees necessary for his defence.

(2) No one shall be held guilty of any penal offence on account of any act or omission which did not constitute a penal offence, under national or international law, at the time when it was committed. Nor shall a heavier penalty be imposed than the one that was applicable at the time the penal offence was committed.

Article 12.

No one shall be subjected to arbitrary interference with his privacy, family, home or correspondence, nor to attacks upon his honour and reputation. Everyone has the right to the protection of the law against such interference or attacks.

Article 13.

(1) Everyone has the right to freedom of movement and residence within the borders of each state.

(2) Everyone has the right to leave any country, including his own, and to return to his country.

Article 14.

(1) Everyone has the right to seek and to enjoy in other countries asylum from persecution.

(2) This right may not be invoked in the case of prosecutions genuinely arising from non-political crimes or from acts contrary to the purposes and principles of the United Nations.

Article 15.

(1) Everyone has the right to a nationality.

(2) No one shall be arbitrarily deprived of his nationality nor denied the right to change his nationality.

Article 16.

(1) Men and women of full age, without any limitation due to race, nationality or religion, have the right to marry and to found a family. They are entitled to equal rights as to

marriage, during marriage and at its dissolution.
(2) Marriage shall be entered into only with the free and full consent of the intending spouses.
(3) The family is the natural and fundamental group unit of society and is entitled to protection by society and the State.

Article 17.

(1) Everyone has the right to own property alone as well as in association with others.

(2) No one shall be arbitrarily deprived of his property.

Article 18.

Everyone has the right to freedom of thought, conscience and religion; this right includes freedom to change his religion or belief, and freedom, either alone or in community with others and in public or private, to manifest his religion or belief in teaching, practice, worship and observance.

Article 19.

Everyone has the right to freedom of opinion and expression; this right includes freedom to hold opinions without interference and to seek, receive and impart information and ideas through any media and regardless of frontiers.

Article 20.

(1) Everyone has the right to freedom of peaceful assembly and association.

(2) No one may be compelled to belong to an association.

Article 21.

(1) Everyone has the right to take part in the government of his country, directly or through freely chosen representatives.

(2) Everyone has the right of equal access to public service in his country.

(3) The will of the people shall be the basis of the authority of government; this will shall be expressed in periodic and genuine elections which shall be by universal and equal suffrage and shall be held by secret vote or by equivalent free voting procedures.

Article 22.

Everyone, as a member of society, has the right to social security and is entitled to realization, through national effort and international co-operation and in accordance with the organization and resources of each State, of the economic, social and cultural rights indispensable for his dignity and the free development of his personality.

Article 23.

(1) Everyone has the right to work, to free choice of employment, to just and favourable conditions of work and to protection against unemployment.

(2) Everyone, without any discrimination, has the right to equal pay for equal work.

(3) Everyone who works has the right to just and favourable remuneration ensuring for himself and his family an existence worthy of human dignity, and supplemented, if necessary, by other means of social protection.

(4) Everyone has the right to form and to join trade unions for the protection of his interests.

Article 24.

Everyone has the right to rest and leisure, including reasonable limitation of working hours and periodic holidays with pay.

Article 25.

(1) Everyone has the right to a standard of living adequate for the health and well-being of himself and of his family, including food, clothing, housing and medical care and necessary social services, and the right to security in the event of unemployment, sickness, disability, widowhood, old age or other lack of livelihood in circumstances beyond his control.

(2) Motherhood and childhood are entitled to special care and assistance. All children, whether born in or out of wedlock, shall enjoy the same social protection.

Article 26.

(1) Everyone has the right to education. Education shall be free, at least in the elementary and fundamental stages. Elementary education shall be compulsory. Technical and professional education shall be made generally available and higher education shall be equally accessible to all on

the basis of merit.

(2) Education shall be directed to the full development of
the human personality and to the strengthening of respect
for human rights and fundamental freedoms. It shall
promote understanding, tolerance and friendship among
all nations, racial or religious groups, and shall further the
activities of the United Nations for the maintenance of
peace.

(3) Parents have a prior right to choose the kind of
education that shall be given to their children.

Article 27.

(1) Everyone has the right freely to participate in the
cultural life of the community, to enjoy the arts and to
share in scientific advancement and its benefits.

(2) Everyone has the right to the protection of the moral
and material interests resulting from any scientific, literary
or artistic production of which he is the author.

Article 28.

Everyone is entitled to a social and international order in
which the rights and freedoms set forth in this Declaration
can be fully realized.

Article 29.

(1) Everyone has duties to the community in which alone
the free and full development of his personality is possible.

(2) In the exercise of his rights and freedoms, everyone

shall be subject only to such limitations as are determined by law solely for the purpose of securing due recognition and respect for the rights and freedoms of others and of meeting the just requirements of morality, public order and the general welfare in a democratic society.

(3) These rights and freedoms may in no case be exercised contrary to the purposes and principles of the United Nations.

Article 30.

Nothing in this Declaration may be interpreted as implying for any State, group or person any right to engage in any activity or to perform any act aimed at the destruction of any of the rights and freedoms set forth herein.

SELECTED ADDITIONAL READINGS

American Association of Physical Anthropologists, "Statement on Race and Racism" adopted March 27, 2019.

Blumrosen, Alfred W. & Ruth G. Blumrosen, *Slave Nation: How Slavery United the Colonies & Sparked the American Revolution* (Naperville, Illinois: Sourcebooks, 2005).

Dobzhansky, Theodosius, *Genetics and the Origin of Species* (New York: Columbia Univ. Press, 1st ed., 1937).

Estes, Kelli, *The Girl Who Wrote in Silk* (Naperville, Illinois: Sourcebooks, 2015).

Fredrickson, George M., *Racism: A Short History* (Princeton, New Jersey: Princeton Univ. Press, 2002).

Fredrickson, George M., *The Arrogance of Race: Historical Perspectives on Slavery, Racism, and Social Inequality* (Hanover, New Hampshire: Wesleyan Univ. Press, 1988).

Hodge, John L., "Democracy and Free Speech: A Normative Theory of Society and Government," Chapter 5 of *The First Amendment Reconsidered*, ed. B. F. Chamberlin & C. J. Brown (New York and London: Longman, 1982).

Hodge, John L., "Equality: Beyond Dualism and Oppression," Chapter 6 of *Anatomy of Racism*, ed. David Theo Goldberg (Minneapolis: Univ. of Minnesota Press, 1990).

Hodge, John L, *How We Are Our Enemy – And How to Stop: Our Unfinished Task of Fulfilling the Values of Democracy* (Jamaica Plain, Mass.: John L. Hodge, Publisher, 2011).

Hodge, John L, *Overcoming the Lie of "Race": A Personal, Philosophical, and Political Perspective*, Second Edition (Jamaica Plain, Mass.: John L. Hodge, Publisher, 2017).

Hodge, John L., Donald K. Struckmann and Lynn Dorland Trost, *Cultural Bases of Racism and Group Oppression: An Examination of Traditional "Western" Concepts, Values and Institutional Structures Which Support Racism, Sexism and Elitism* (Berkeley, Calif.: Two Riders Press, 1975). Part I and Part IV of this book are reprinted in *Race and Culture in America*, 3rd edition, ed. C. E. Jackson and E. J. Tolbert (Edina MN: Burgess International Group, 1989).

Hunt, Lynn, *Inventing Human Rights* (New York: W. W. Norton & Co., 2007).

Irving, Debby, *Waking Up White: And Finding Myself in the Story of Race* (Cambridge, Mass.: Elephant Room Press, 2014).

Jones, Jacqueline, *A Dreadful Deceit: The Myth of Race from the Colonial Era to Obama's America* (New York: Basic Books, 2013).

Krimsky, Sheldon and Kathleen Sloan, ed., *Race and the Genetic Revolution: Science, Myth, and Culture* (New York: Columbia Univ. Press, 2011).

Loving v. *Virginia*, 388 U.S. 1 (1967).

Montagu, Ashley, *Man's Most Dangerous Myth: The Fallacy of Race*, 4th ed. (Cleveland: World Pub. Co., 1964); 1st ed. originally published in 1942; sixth ed. (Lanham, Maryland: AltaMira Press, 1997).

Montagu, Ashley, "The Meaninglessness of the Anthropological Conception of Race," *The Journal of Heredity*, Vol. 23, 1941, pp. 243-247.

Northrup, F. S. C., *The Meeting of East and West* (New York: Macmillan, 1960) (originally published in 1946).

Ortega y Gasset, Jose, *The Modern Theme*, trans. J. Cleugh (New York: Harper Torchbooks, 1961) (originally published in 1923 as *Tema de nuestro tiempo*).

Oswalt, Wendell H., *This Land Was Theirs: A Study of the North American Indian* (New York: John Wiley & Sons, 1966).

Partanen, Anu, *The Nordic Theory of Everything* (New York: HarperCollins, 2016).

Pascoe, Peggy, *What Comes Naturally: Miscegenation Law and the Making of Race in America* (New York: Oxford Univ. Press, 2009).

Rodney, Walter, *How Europe Underdeveloped Africa* (Washington, D.C.: Howard Univ. Press, 1974).

Sharfstein, Daniel J., *The Invisible Line: A Secret History of Race in America* (New York: Penguin Group, 2011).

Sykes, Byran, *DNA USA: A Genetic Portrait of America* (New York: Liveright Pub., 2012).

tenBroek, Jacobus, et al., *Prejudice, War and the Constitution* (Berkeley: Univ. of California Press, 1970).

Wattles, Jeffrey, *The Golden Rule* (New York & Oxford: Oxford Univ. Press, 1996).

Whitehead, Alfred North, *Science and the Modern World* (New York: Macmillan, 1967) (originally published in 1925).

Whitman, James Q, *Hitler's American Model: The United States and the Making of Nazi Race Law* (Princeton: Princeton Univ. Press, 2017).

Wood, Betty, *The Origins of American Slavery* (New York: Hill and Wang, 1997).

THE AUTHOR

John L. Hodge's writings consist of books, book chapters, letters and a blog that pave the way towards a more humane society. He is the principal co-author of *Cultural Bases of Racism and Group Oppression: An Examination of Traditional "Western" Concepts, Values and Institutional Structures Which Support Racism, Sexism and Elitism* (1975). He is the author of "Democracy and Free Speech: A Normative Theory of Society and Government," Chapter 5 of *The First Amendment Reconsidered* (1982); "Equality: Beyond Dualism and Oppression," Chapter 6 of *Anatomy of Racism* (1990); *How We Are Our Enemy — And How to Stop: Our Unfinished Task of Fulfilling the Values of Democracy* (2011); *Dialogues on God: Three Views* (2012), and *Overcoming the Lie of "Race": A Personal, Philosophical, and Political Perspective* (2017 — 2nd ed.).

He has an A.B. in mathematics from the University of Kansas (where he was awarded membership into Phi Beta Kappa), a Ph.D. in philosophy from Yale University, and a law degree (J.D.) from the University of California, Berkeley (Berkeley Law). In his long career beginning in the mid-1960s he was a draft counselor and peace intern with the American Friends Service Committee in Houston and Seattle; a college teacher and university professor mostly at California State University, East Bay; a Law Clerk for the Massachusetts Appeals Court; a Staff Attorney for the U. S. Court of Appeals for the First Circuit; and a lawyer for Massachusetts state agencies that provided health care, including Medicaid. He participated in the development of the Massachusetts model that was used nationally to create the Affordable Care Act (known as "Obamacare"). He lives with his wife in the Boston area.

For more information, go to http://JohnLHodge.com.